Believing Bishops

by Simon Lee
Law and Morals
Judging Judges

by Peter Stanford
Hidden Hands: Child Workers
around the World

Believing Bishops

Simon Lee and Peter Stanford

faber and faber

LONDON · BOSTON

First published in 1990
by Faber and Faber Limited
3 Queen Square London WC1N 3AU

Photoset by Parker Typesetting Service Leicester
Printed in Great Britain by
Richard Clay Ltd Bungay Suffolk

© Simon Lee and Peter Stanford, 1990

A CIP record for this book is available from the
British Library

ISBN 0–571–14191–9

*To our parents with
love and thanks for
their support*

Contents

_____

Preface

Believe it or not, indeed believe them or not, busy bishops have devoted hours to being interviewed by us. Unbelievably, we have busied ourselves in researching the role of bishops, interviewing their worst enemies, reading the work of their biographers and studying dry church texts. Why do they and we think the effort has been worth while?

First, all the bishops agreed that there was a need for such a book. They were unaware of any similar attempt to analyse their role. Second, we were conscious that the popular media and even serious social and political commentators fail to understand the role of religion in our lives. Anthony Sampson's influential book *The Changing Anatomy of Britain*, for example, omits the bishops and churches altogether. Even Hugo Young's monumental account of the Thatcher years allocates a mere 5 out of 550 pages to the bishops.

Yet in our professional lives we encounter the influence of bishops constantly. One of us, as the editor of a religious newspaper, is continually assessing bishops and is increasingly asked by fellow journalists to predict who will be the next Archbishops of Canterbury and Westminster. The questioners want a couple of names. The answer is that they really need a couple of hundred pages about bishops. Here they are.

The other co-author, as a professor of jurisprudence, is increasingly asked whether the law ought to be a no-go zone for bishops. The answer given here is that there should be no no-go zones for bishops although their interventions in private morality, law and politics would benefit from being approached with the fearful tread of angels rather than the fools' rush.

In our own professions, we have been fortunate enough to be

entrusted with responsibility at an early age. This never happens, sadly, with bishops. Bishops inhabit a world of old men and many who write about them are oldish men, often also of a clerical (or ex-clerical) background. We hope that this book offers a fresh look at religion from the perspective of a younger generation and in plain, some would say irreverent, language.

We wanted to explore the inside story, to understand how the bishops themselves see their own role. We have quoted extensively from our interviews with the bishops, reporting them verbatim to convey the fact that we were in conversation. Their prose may not, therefore, be as polished or grammatical as usual. We hope they will forgive us for this minor sin and for the cardinal sin of doubting bishops and even cardinals.

We are grateful to them for their help. Those who know bishops best are their wives (in the case of Anglicans), their clerical secretaries and their clergy. All three groups, and especially the rank and file priests, have expressed strong views to us which we have incorporated without due acknowledgement so as to protect their relationships with their bishops. We would also like to thank our other 'informants' from politicians to journalists and to the people in the pews.

There are two non-acknowledgements. Although one of us has a brother who is a priest and although a former colleague of one of us is now a bishop and a leading contender to be the next Archbishop of Canterbury, we have thought it right to spare them embarrassment and thus not to consult them at all. They cannot be blamed for what follows.

As for positive acknowledgements, we are very grateful to Clare Rooney, Sharon Thompson, The Queen's University of Belfast, the *Catholic Herald*, British Airways, British Midland and Fax for overcoming the difficulties of producing the manuscript from either side of the Irish Sea. We have received every encouragement from Will Sulkin and his colleagues at Faber and Faber who have also shown considerable patience.

Our families and friends have been supportive above and beyond the call of duty: Patricia, Jamie, Katie and Rebecca Lee, Deborah Thomas and Joanna Moorhead deserve particular thanks for all their help. We dedicate this book to our parents for, we suppose, bringing us up to believe in bishops.

Part I

Ancient and Modern

———

1

Bishops Beyond Belief?

———

Who will succeed Robert Runcie as the next Archbishop of Canterbury? Who will succeed Basil Hume as the next Archbishop of Westminster? Does anybody care? If media headlines are anything to go by, the public is interested. But does our supposedly secular society really listen to the bishops? Why should anybody take notice of what celibate Catholic bishops have to say about sex? Why should anyone pay any attention to what those pillars of the establishment, Anglican bishops living in their rural palaces, think about unemployment in the inner city? Why should non-believers believe anything the bishops have to say, especially when some bishops (notably the Bishop of Durham) are themselves constantly questioning the fundamental notions of religious belief?

This book seeks to answer these and other related questions. In Chapter 3, we shall support our claim that the media are increasingly interested in what Anglican and Catholic bishops have to say about all manner of controversies. In the last year, for example, there was intense press and television coverage of the bishops' views on subjects in which they could hardly be considered experts, such as extradition and the poll tax. The media also found space for internal church matters, such as episcopal reinterpretations of Christ's ascension, the issue of blasphemy in the wake of Salman Rushdie's book *The Satanic Verses*, and the appointment of the first woman as an Anglican bishop.

But it is not obvious *why* the media want to know bishops' views on all these topics. It is also far from clear why the bishops have taken up the invitations to offer their opinions to a national audience, given that some of the subject matter seems a long way away from traditional ideas of religion's place. The media are quick to respond by condemning bishops in political terms as too liberal or too conservative, or more straightforwardly as good or bad, yet without really appreciating or even questioning what a bishop's role is or should be. We have, therefore, asked the bishops themselves what they think they are doing. We have sought to analyse what they have already done. We have suggested what they might do in the future.

Speculation on the type of bishop that we need is given extra significance by the impending changes at the top of the English churches. In the very near future, Robert Runcie will retire as Archbishop of Canterbury. In the not-too-distant future, Basil Hume will at least try to retire as Cardinal Archbishop of Westminster (although he promised at his installation in 1976 to remain no more than ten years in office). Who will succeed them?

We propose to answer this question by building up a picture of the kind of bishop most needed by today's churches. We should stress at the very outset of this quest that it would be wrong to seek one model for all bishops. Bishops form a team, or more technically a synod or a conference, which can and does resemble a football team in having both attackers and defenders of the faith, together with midfield schemers. Not everybody can play in the same position if the team is to function. Indeed, the geography of the football pitch, or of the country at large, dictates that some will play on the right and some on the left. Depending on the state of the nation and especially on the state of the nation's faith, different kinds of leaders are needed.

A second preliminary qualification is that the bishops themselves and their fellow believers will maintain that the Holy Spirit is at work in choosing bishops and that what might be called the Becket syndrome can transform an unlikely choice into a vigorous conscience of the nation. Bishops can grow into their office, as illustrated by the dramatic transformation in Archbishop Oscar Romero of San Salvador who on appointment in 1977 seemed to be yet another conservative but who rapidly emerged as a paradigm voice of the voiceless to the point of martyrdom three years later.

A third point to stress in relation to the appointment of bishops is that we, the people, can have our say. Both Anglican and Catholic traditions have the machinery to allow the laity to make suggestions to the appropriate authorities. Christians ought to take that opportunity seriously, to reflect on it responsibly and to regard it as a moral or theological duty just as much as most of us see it as important to exercise our right to vote in political elections. Of course, the churches do not hold a ballot when appointing a bishop (although they more or less did in the early church) and cynics would claim that the easiest way to damn a candidate's chances would be for the laity to put his name forward. But so-called 'leading laymen' are already playing this game and a more representative picture of public opinion ought to be presented to those who make such important decisions.

We would regard this book as a success if readers are prompted into discussing the kind of leaders they want for their churches and then if they make those views known to the powers that be. We do not intend to prejudice the chances of individual clerics or the minds of readers by merely giving a detailed form guide on the likely runners. Instead, we propose to examine the nature of the bishops' role in the church from a variety of perspectives, beginning naturally enough with the very beginning of the Christian church.

There is biblical authority for a three-fold episcopal role at the very end of St Matthew's Gospel (Matthew 28, 16–20):

> The eleven disciples made their way to Galilee, to the mountain where Jesus had told them to meet him. When they saw him, they fell prostrate before him, though some were doubtful. Jesus then came up and spoke to them. He said: 'Full authority in heaven and on earth has been committed to me. Go forth therefore and make all nations my disciples; baptize men everywhere in the name of the Father and the Son and the Holy Spirit, and teach them to observe all that I have commanded you. And be assured, I am with you always, to the end of time.'

In the New Testament, then, bishops are seen as teachers, as 'sanctifiers' and as pastors. In the original context of the twelve apostles, it is relatively easy to see how St Peter and his friends could educate their followers in the good news, could bless the activities of their communities and could act as good shepherds to their own flocks. But in the modern world, where bishops run banks (Marcinkus), circumnavigate the globe (John Paul II), employ press officers (Richard Harries), challenge governments (Tutu) and are identified in the public's mind with their *Spitting Image* puppets (Runcie), it is difficult to see what common threads run through their lives. What exactly is it that they are meant to teach – the gospels, controversial economic theories, politics, social ethics? Should they be using modern media (e.g. the video link or satellite TV) to show their people that they are indeed blessing them as they administer the sacraments? In what practical sense can they act as pastors to the millions under their spiritual care, or is that role simply symbolic?

Apart from public interest, there are two signs of the times which suggest to us that a detailed examination of the episcopal role is much needed. First, in all manner of countries around the world, bishops are picking up the mantle of opposition to governments. Even in the United Kingdom this is the case. For the last decade Margaret Thatcher's control of the country has been impervious to criticism from the Labour party and the various groupings within the centre of British politics. But, from time to time, it has been the bishops who have publicly challenged her authority. Why is it that the bishops have become the voice of the voiceless, not only in places such as El Salvador but even in England?

Secondly, why is it that there has been a growing question as to the commitment of British bishops to their own faith? Most spec-tacularly, the Bishop of Durham has continued to act as if he were an academic theologian, probing the nature of faith but laying himself open to the charge of misleading the faithful.

We hope to show that these reasons for interest (media activity, opposition to governments, questions of belief) are interrelated. The media are interested because they see a story in any challenge to the government. They also regard the clergy as a relic of a religious past and so are endlessly amused by prelates themselves questioning the intricacies of some simplistic religious belief. Yet this willingness to update, paradoxically, makes the bishops seem more acceptable to secular sceptics, so that liberal critics of the government are nowa-days more prepared to invoke the aid of bishops.

The media, of course, love personalities. The Catholic and Angli-can traditions supply identifiable figure-heads in their bishops. Thus, the papers are interested in what the Catholic and Anglican bishops of Liverpool have to say, but that dynamic duo's efforts to include the Free Churches Moderator in their crusades always fail because the Free Churches eschew personality cults.

Part I of this book seeks to establish the contemporary signifi-cance of bishops, then explores different models for today's bishops in scripture and church tradition. Part II looks at some of the issues facing today's bishops and assesses their response. Part III examines the personalities among our bishops and attempts to draw out common threads. Finally, Part IV looks towards the challenges of the next decade and the next millennium in choosing tomorrow's bishops.

This structure and the title of this book echo the first-named author's recent book, *Judging Judges*. Just as the judiciary are a target of media caricature and needed to have their role explained, so we are now looking at another important part of British public and private life which merits examination. The judiciary are criticized for being old, white, male, rich, upper middle-class, public school and Oxbridge. So too are bishops. Both groups are attacked for interfering in politics. Yet their jobs take them inexorably into the issues and areas which politicians in turn regard as their preserve.

But bishops, if they are to be believed, should not be simply another part of the establishment like the judges. If we are to believe in their office, they have to convince us that they do have a distinct part to play in our lives, a part which is qualitatively different from those played by various officers of the state.

What, then, is that special element? We must, of course, distinguish two different kinds of question about the role of bishops in society. First, we might ask what bishops do. Second, we might ask what bishops ought to do. The answer to the latter is a standard by which to judge their performance in answer to the first question. It is the answer to the second question which is more important, which should set the agenda for the bishops of tomorrow. For bishops are only human: they will inevitably fail to measure up to any idealized standard. If we rake over past mistakes, this does not condemn the authority of bishops, but rather highlights the human failings of past practice. Of bishops in particular, as G. K. Chesterton wrote of Christianity in general: 'the trouble with Christianity is not that it has been tried and found wanting but that it has been wanted and never tried.' Similarly, we might conclude that there really is a distinct role for bishops but one which is only too rarely fulfilled.

If we have to single out just one quality which makes bishops such a fascinating subject, it might be found in the title of a book written by the present Pope. He called his series of meditations on the role of priests *A Sign of Contradiction*. Of course, many malcontents, from the disturbed to the anarchic, could count as signs of contradiction. But what Pope John Paul II meant was that priests in general, and we would add bishops in particular, ought to be challenging their flocks through the example of their own lives. They should not be assimilated into the material, temporal order. If we are to believe bishops, then their belief must call us to a different way of life, a different set of values. In a Christ-like way, they should be guiding us to the spiritual order. There is, therefore, a great danger in judging bishops by conventional, secular standards. We might be forgiven for worrying, however, whether some bishops believe that themselves.

We hope that this book will also act as a catalyst for wider reflection about the place of religion in contemporary society. Bishops are symbols. An exploration of their lives may help us understand more clearly the nature of religious belief. It may be that the answer to the question why our secular society listens to the bishops lies in querying whether our society really is secular. 'Secular', in this context, means sceptical of religious truth. It may be that society is instead sceptical of irreligious, materialistic 'truth'. Society may be awaiting spiritual leadership, sensing that there is more to life than politicians can provide, but not knowing where to start on a pilgrimage towards religious belief. Thus, we hope that this book may help both those who are wondering whether to believe their bishops and those who are wondering whether their bishops believe.

2

The Basis for Believing Bishops

―

Christianity

We can only appreciate the role of bishops if we have some idea of the faith they profess. Above all, Christianity offers a model for our lives, the model of Christ's life. Christians believe not just in what Christ said but in what he did and what he was. Whereas Marxists do not have to condone the private life of Karl Marx, to Christians the private and public life of Christ is precisely their belief.

So Christians believe that they should go through life behaving, in so far as they can, in a Christ-like manner. Why? There are two reasons in practice. One is shared by many non-Christians and perhaps explains secular interest in today's bishops. Some people try to live their lives in a Christ-like way simply because they think of Christ as a good man. A second group go further and say that they follow Christ because he was not just a good man but also the Son of God.

One test for Christians then, in any situation, is to ask themselves what Christ would have done. But there is a further test, not just acting like Christ but also acting as if we were doing something *to* Christ. The scriptural authority for this is clear: 'Whatever you do unto these the least of my children, you do unto me.' So Christians are meant to see Christ in the people around them, they are meant to behave towards tramps, lepers, terrorists, enemies, indeed all and sundry, as if they were Christ. Of course, in the unlikely event that Christians and others really did behave in a Christ-like way, the world would be a transformed and infinitely better place. That's the point.

Now why do we need a church or bishops to help us in the Christian life? The idea is not, despite popular belief, to make things more difficult for the Christian. On the contrary, bishops and the churches are there to help individual Christians work out the meaning of their beliefs for their individual lives. Mother Teresa has put this well. She begins her day by taking communion at Mass, seeing Christ in the Host, which prepares her for her work amongst the poor, sick, despised and destitute. After participating in the universal church's eucharistic rite, she feels strengthened and encouraged to see Christ in her fellow human beings. And if somebody like Mother Teresa, who is often described as a living saint, needs such help, then no wonder that Christ felt the need to appoint his apostles to the specific task of teaching, caring for and sanctifying his flock.

New Testament Texts for Bishops

From Jesus Christ to the landmark liberalizing Second Vatican Council of the Catholic church in the 1960s, bishops have been asked to teach, to sanctify and to guide. Several bishops referred us to John, Chapter 10, verses 14–16:

> I am the good shepherd; I know my own sheep and my sheep know me – as the Father knows me and I know the Father – and I lay down my life for the sheep. But there are other sheep of mine not belonging to this fold whom I must bring in; and they too will listen to my voice. There will then be one flock, one shepherd.

But this has to be linked to the end of St John's Gospel (John, Chapter 21, verse 15): 'Jesus said to Simon Peter, "Simon, Son of John, do you love me more than all else?" "Yes, Lord," he answered, "you know that I love you." "Then feed my lambs," he said.'

Another vital text, especially for Catholic bishops, is Matthew, Chapter 16, verse 18: 'You are Peter, the Rock; and upon this rock I will build my church, and the powers of death shall never conquer it. I will give you the keys of the Kingdom of Heaven; what you forbid on earth shall be forbidden in heaven and what you allow on earth shall be allowed in heaven.'

But if we look in the rest of the New Testament, the emphasis is not so much on the duties of the bishop as on his personal qualities. In St Paul's First Letter to Timothy, Chapter 3, verses 2–7 run as follows:

> Our leader, therefore, or Bishop, must be above reproach, faithful to his one wife, sober, temperate, courteous, hospitable,

and a good teacher; he must not be driven to drink, or a brawler, but of a forbearing disposition, avoiding quarrels, and no lover of money. He must be one who manages his own household well and wins obedience from his children, and a man of the highest principles. If a man does not know how to control his own family, how can he look after a congregation of God's people? He must not be a convert newly baptised, for fear the sin of conceit should bring upon him a judgement contrived by the devil. He must, moreover, have a good reputation with a non-Christian public, so that he may not be exposed to scandal and get caught in the devil's snare.

'Bishop' is probably not being used here in our modern, technical sense, for St Paul is reflecting on Christian leadership in general. Nevertheless, it will be seen from that list that the earliest bishops were married men with families, as indeed is obvious from the rest of the New Testament in which, for instance, Peter's mother-in-law features prominently. Yet today's Catholic bishops are celibate. And some Anglican and Catholic bishops do not measure up to the qualities in the rest of the list either.

For present purposes, however, what is important is that from the earliest days of the church there is a recognizable role of bishop. But although the office dates back to Christ's commissioning of Peter and the apostles, he did not lay down precise rules for the episcopal order. These have rather been worked out by the church over the past 2,000 years. In the first century after Christ there seems to have been both an episcopal order and a presbyterial order. The latter is probably the immediate successor to the twelve apostles, in that the idea consists of a council of leaders co-operating in the running of a local Christian community. In contrast, the Pauline concept of apostleship suggests that the risen Lord is represented by a single apostle, or later by a single bishop.

Bishops in the Early Church

By the end of the first century a monarchical view of the bishop's role had emerged. It is of a single man, acting as the representative of Christ, who forms the focus of unity in a local church, albeit in communion with other churches. By the middle of the second century, there was a shift back from the Christocentric theology of the bishop to recognition of the bishops in general as successors to the apostles.

Later, the church fathers' formulation of the bishop's duties included preaching the gospel, conducting worship (e.g. ordaining priests, which other priests cannot do), exercising discipline (e.g. by excommunicating) and generally serving Christ in building up his church. From the fourth century an extra dimension began to receive renewed significance: namely, each bishop's responsibility for the church as a whole (e.g. the fact the bishops concelebrate at a consecration of another bishop, the issuing of encyclicals, the holding of synods and council). The Bishop of Rome was seen as the most direct successor of Peter, guaranteeing the universal unity of the church through this process.

Bishops in the Medieval Church

By the tenth century, we can see an East–West division, with the patriarchs of the Eastern church perhaps keeping the faith better than the increasingly dictatorial rulers of the Western church. Once Pope John X acknowledged in AD 921 the right of states to appoint bishops, they began to be seen as princes of empires, of medieval states. This secularization of the episcopacy proved to be dangerous for the church. In the eleventh century, of course, various popes attempted to separate church and state precisely to safeguard episcopal autonomy. This in turn created problems, particularly in that the Bishop of Rome was given increased significance, which caused difficulties during the weakness of the successive popes of the fourteenth century.

Reformation Bishops

Eventually, in the sixteenth century, the Reformation produced a challenge to the secularization of the bishops. The Reformation, in effect, pushed aside those bishops who had become a source of scandal owing to their delight in the temporal rather than the spiritual order. This caused Catholic theologians to work out a refined vision of the episcopacy, focusing on the pastoral dimension. As Wolfgang Beinert has written: 'Bishops were exalted to care for their flocks in an apostolic spirit. Sixteenth-century writers inspired by the Council of Trent described the ideal bishop as a likeness of the Good Shepherd, a likeness that became flesh and blood in such men as St Charles Borromeo and St Francis de Sales.'

Modern Bishops – The Catholic Liturgical Basis

Unfortunately, the First Vatican Council ended prematurely in 1870, without time to complete its task of developing a thorough-going theology of the episcopacy. So the task was left to the Second Vatican Council in the 1960s. That Council concentrated on the sacramental basis of becoming a bishop, the collegiality – collective responsibility – of the bishops under the Pope, in short the connections between the local churches and the universal church.

The Second Vatican Council makes clear the Catholic church's view that we need to understand the New Testament in order to understand today's bishops: 'Just as by the Lord's will, St Peter and the other apostles constituted one apostolic college, so in a similar way the Roman Pontiff as the successor of Peter, and the bishops as the successors of the apostles, are joined together.' The Council insisted that Christ is present and active among his bishops: 'In the bishops our Lord Jesus Christ the Supreme High Priest is present in the midst of those who believe.' How so? 'This sacred synod teaches that by episcopal consecration is conferred a fullness of the sacrament of orders.'

The liturgical rite of episcopal consecration involves prayer and the laying on of hands, signifying the gift of special grace in order to fulfil a special task. The prayers ask for the new bishop to be given that power of the Spirit which Christ had given to his apostles, for the grace necessary to guide the universal church. All the bishops present at an episcopal consecration impose their hands on the newly elected bishop. Thus, it is not one bishop consecrating his successor but rather it is the entire college of bishops who welcome a new member. This consolidates the structure of the Catholic church so that the bishops remain 'linked with one another and with the Bishop of Rome by the bonds of unity, charity and peace'. There is, however, no doubt in Catholic theology that one bishop is the first among equals: 'The Roman Pontiff, as the successor of Peter, is the perpetual and visible source and foundation of the unity of the bishops and of the multitude of the faithful. The individual bishop, however, is the visible principle and foundation of unity in his particular church, fashioned after the model of the universal church. In and from such individual churches there comes into being the one and only Catholic church.'

The point to stress here is the liturgical basis for believing bishops. For example, Basil Hume's ordination as a bishop in Westminster Cathedral was a significant liturgical moment. Catholic bishops are usually ordained in Rome. Moreover, Abbot Hume was the first priest in England and Wales to be ordained directly as the bishop of a diocese since the liturgical rite was revised, in the wake of the Second Vatican Council's deeper understanding of the bishops' role.

The most important part of the ordination came, as we have already indicated, when all the concelebrating bishops laid their hands on the head of Basil Hume. This is the action which the apostles themselves used to set apart those who were to carry on their work, the work of Christ himself as teacher and shepherd – sanctifying, teaching and governing his flock. The laying on of hands was done in complete silence to attract the whole attention of the congregation. Its symbolism, that of the continuity of apostolic succession, is the basis for following bishops, even when one does not quite believe them.

The next element in the liturgy was the consecratory prayer, which dates from the third century and is still used in some of the Eastern churches such as the Coptic rite. Again, all the consecrating bishops recited the prayer, which emphasizes the spirit of leadership given by God the Father to his Son, Jesus Christ, a spirit which Christ passed on to the apostles and which was now being passed on to Basil Hume.

Then the head of the new bishop was anointed with oil, originally to stress the role of the bishop in the ministry of reconciliation, as a peacemaker. In the new rite, the anointing is seen more as a reference to the Old Testament tradition of anointing the High Priest.

Next, the book of gospels was held over Basil Hume's head, to emphasize his new episcopal responsibility as principal teacher of his flock. Then he was given his ring, mitre and crozier. The ring signifies that the bishop is wedded to Christ. The mitre does not really signify anything at all; it has been the distinctive head-covering of bishops since the twelfth century but has no biblical roots. The crozier (or crook or staff) is, in contrast, redolent with symbolism. It is the chief sign that the bishop is to be the shepherd of his flock.

The first duty of the apostles, according to the passage from Matthew quoted earlier (p. 5) was to teach all nations. By the gift of grace which the bishop receives at his consecration, he is given a 'special charism of truth' comparable to that which the apostles received at Pentecost. Catholic bishops have often emphasized their responsibility to exclude all error from the teaching of the church. It is this which has led to controversy in the Catholic church over the rights and duties of theologians as compared to bishops, a dispute to which we will return later.

The sacramental role of the bishops is not easy to explain or for non-believers to understand. The bishops are seen as the principal ministers of the sacraments, helped by their priests. St Thomas Aquinas puts this well:

> It pertains to the bishop to give simple priests what is necessary for the fulfilment of their proper function. That is why the blessing of the Holy Chrism, of the Oil of Catechumens, of altars of churches, of vestments and of sacred vessels ... is reserved to the bishop as head of the whole ecclesiastical order.

On Maundy Thursday this is most clearly seen, as the priests of a diocese come together to the cathedral, to receive the holy chrism and oils from their bishop and to renew their ordination vows.

As pastor of his church, a bishop is expected to govern or administer his diocese. Church documents refer to him, in this regard, as 'the vicar of Christ' or an 'ambassador of Christ'. The bishop is to have pastoral care especially for his priests, who themselves then care for the laity. Many of the bishops take this responsibility to be their most special task, that of caring for their clergy.

Modern Bishops – The Anglican Liturgical Basis

The similarity between Basil Hume's consecration and the service for an Archbishop of Canterbury is not surprising, since the induction of the Archbishop of Westminster is based on the rite used at Canterbury in the early fifteenth century. At the beginning of the ceremony, the Dean of the cathedral prayed for the new archbishop that 'by God's grace you may govern and guide this See to which the eyes of all Anglican Christians look as the centre of their Communion and fellowship'. That prayer will be all the more poignant next time as the issue of women bishops threatens to fragment the Anglican communion. Robert Runcie's service was catholic (in the sense of cosmopolitan), involving representatives of other denominations and faiths from around the world. Thus, not only Cardinal Hume but also the Anglican Archbishop of West Africa and the Orthodox Archbishop of Thyateira participated. Perhaps the most moving moment for all the bishops present and for the millions around the world watching the service on television or listening on the radio, came when the saints and martyrs were remembered: to the usual litany of names was added that of Oscar Romero, the Roman Catholic Archbishop of San Salvador, who had been assassinated as he said Mass the day before.

It will come as no surprise to any follower of bishops' sermons that Robert Runcie began his arch-episcopal preaching by claiming that he had had a dream. In a later chapter we will see that Cardinal Hume had a dream about the church as a pilgrim. Equally significantly, his critics would argue, Archbishop Runcie's dream was about being lost in a maze:

> I long to be able to speak while archbishop with men and women who stand outside the Christ church. I would like to say to them, 'You can teach us so much if together we could look for the secret of the maze-like muddle in which the world finds itself.' I ask for your prayers that I may be given the grace to speak like that and to listen . . .

More importantly, and powerfully, Archbishop Runcie laid down the battle lines with politicians during the Thatcher years:

> The cry is 'the church must give a firm lead'. Yes, it must – a firm lead against rigid thinking, a judging temper of mind, the disposition to over-simplify the difficult and complex problems. If the church gives Jesus Christ's sort of lead it will not be popular. It may even be despised for failing to grasp the power which is offered to it in the confusion and fears of our contemporaries.

If we are right in claiming that the theological basis for believing bishops is best illustrated by the liturgy at their consecration services and that there is much in common between the Anglican and Catholic rites, then perhaps all is not lost for Christian unity. In the case of Cardinal Hume and Archbishop Runcie they have the same anniversary, their consecrations having taken place on 25 March (1976 and 1980 respectively). Cardinal Hume's day is remembered as being the feast of the Annunciation. Archbishop Runcie's chosen date became memorable when Sir Geoffrey Howe announced that it would also be budget day. The media interpreted this as a snub, instead of a *faux pas* (the snubs were to come later, once the government and the Anglican bishops were set on a collision course). The Leader of the House of Commons, Norman St John Stevas (who was thought by many, not least himself, to be a far more suitable Archbishop of Westminster or Canterbury, and who had earlier worked hard behind the scenes to fulfil his prediction that Worlock would become Archbishop of Liverpool and Hume Archbishop of Westminster), later told the House that the budget would be moved to the Wednesday.

Given the gibes about the increasingly politicized bishops being more interested in rates of unemployment than the rights or wrongs of anything religious, it was a minor triumph that the budget and not the Canterbury enthronement was moved.

In the topsy-turvy world of bishops and Ministers, we might be forgiven for imagining that Robert Runcie busied himself in the days before his enthronement by appointing his Cabinet Ministers, in contrast to Mrs Thatcher, who responded to her appointment with a prayer (some say outrageously hijacking St Francis of Assisi's best lines). Well, Runcie did use this time to appoint Terry Waite, an inspired choice, as his Foreign Secretary. But he also prepared for his spiritual post with spiritual exercises. He spent the day before the ceremony praying with the other Anglican primates who had flown in for the service.

But what was he praying about? Undoubtedly, for the grace to lead and sanctify his flock. This notion of 'sanctifying' is also difficult for the non-believer to understand. It is pretty difficult for the believer to comprehend, one might add. But the basic idea is illustrated by the Second Vatican Council's explanation of the way in which the eucharistic sacrament and the associated liturgy of the Mass sanctify those who participate:

The liturgy is thus the outstanding means by which the faithful can express in their lives, and manifest to others, the mystery of Christ and the real nature of the true church. It is of the essence of the church that she be both human and divine, visible and yet invisibly endowed, eager to act and yet devoted to contemplation, present in this world and yet not at home in it . . . Day by day the liturgy builds up those within the church into the Lord's holy temple . . . At the same time the liturgy marvellously fortifies the faithful in their capacity to preach Christ. To outsiders the liturgy thereby reveals the church as a sign raised above the nations. Under this sign the scattered sons of God are being gathered into one until there is one fold and one shepherd.

The other sacraments also build up the believer at key times during his or her life, at baptism, in marriage, when facing death, and so on. It is part of the bishops' role to ensure this sanctification of their flock.

*

It should be clear from this potted summary of the Christian faith that bishops are important symbols of Christ-in-action. Indeed, the regalia of their office make this clear – for example, the shepherd's crook is an obvious sign to the world of the pastoral role laid down for his successors by the Good Shepherd. If we are to believe in bishops, therefore, they have to be living examples of Christian belief and Christ-like actions. In the words of St Thomas Aquinas, 'It is the duty of bishops to be perfect and teachers of perfection.'

3

More than Media Megastars

––––

The bishops are much more than a relic of a religious past. Nowadays it seems impossible to open any national newspaper, or follow the news on any television or radio channel, without somewhere finding a bishop preaching to millions on a subject about which he seems singularly ill-equipped to pontificate. No longer are our leading churchmen content with an occasional supporting role on the inside pages, being literally a Godsend to picture editors because of their fancy dress. Today it is the bishops who are making the headlines, even dominating the front pages.

The bishops are well aware that this is sometimes simply because the press want to use them. As the Archbishop of York told us:

> Newspapers continually carry articles 'Archbishop Raps', 'Bishop Speaks Out On' and usually what that means is that some enterprising reporter has rung up that morning and said that this has happened, what do you think of it. And if you're unwise you'll launch into a statement.

Even that media star, the Bishop of Durham, was conscious of this and assured us – some would say flying in the face of considerable evidence – that 'I will not be a rent-a-quote'.

Nowadays the faces of our prelates have also become familiar through television. Nor do they appear only in the traditional 'God-slots', after midnight or early on a Sunday evening, when the two major television channels pay lip-service to their religious obligations with sugary compilations of hymns-you-love-to-hate. Now it's the nine or ten o'clock news which is more likely to feature a bishop.

What has brought about this media stardom? The bishops themselves put it down to the changing nature of society – most notably the advent of Margaret Thatcher as Prime Minister and the dramatic, and to many unsettling, effects that her radical policies have had on national life. It is in such times of social and economic upheaval, the prelates' argument runs, that society as a whole – active churchgoers or not – turns towards something more stable, enduring, predictable and spiritual. That is what the church can provide and it has responded vigorously to the summons.

But the prominence of bishops and their opinions on today's issues is not in fact a new phenomenon. Throughout the ages people have listened to the bishops in their times of need, of doubt, when familiar notions are being challenged.

It may be that the growing prosperity of the post-war years diminished that hunger for the church's guidance. If so, however, reaction to the policies of Margaret Thatcher reawakened the traditional role: 'The post-war political consensus, which had been deeply influenced by the Christian faith, has been attacked in the Thatcher years on a number of fronts,' according to the Anglican Bishop of Manchester, Stanley Booth-Clibborn. He and his fellow clerics have responded to that onslaught on behalf , they claim, of their congregations, spurred on by the fears and worries they have heard voiced by their flocks. Jointly and individually the bishops have 'gone public' repeatedly on a whole range of topics, from the inner cities, through the poll tax and employment legislation, to local government conduct and even bus deregulation.

To those Cabinet Ministers who continue to claim that bishops have no business 'poking their noses into politics', the clerics respond with rare unanimity that they only speak out when an issue obliges them as Christian leaders to do so. David Jenkins, the Bishop of Durham – a favourite target for critics within the Conservative party who like to divert attention from the substance of bishops' interventions by dubbing them 'loony, lefty churchmen' – explains his attitude this way:

> I don't go round looking for chances to speak in this 'I'm making a statement' sense. You only do it because things address you. And that's how things started, for example, with my involvement in the miners' strike. It seemed to me clear, quite apart from the long tradition of the bishops of Durham with the mining community, that if you're going to speak in a

great and ancient cathedral you cannot avoid addressing one of the most painful living issues that we were then in the midst of. And I came to the conclusion that if you're going to address it, you've got to say something specific and controversial. A friend of mine once said that bishops are, generally speaking, generally speaking. The down-to-earthness of God can be extremely uncomfortable, and it's not up to me to make it comfortable. It's certainly not up to me to set out to make people uncomfortable, but there are times when any sort of preaching or speaking must engage at a point where it might hurt.

It is not simply the fact that the bishops have entered or re-entered the political debate in the Thatcher years that has angered Ministers and prompted widespread media attention; rather, it is the comprehensive and detailed nature of the bishops' rejection both of the substance of government policy and of the philosophy that underpins it. In October 1987, for example, Bishop Jenkins told the Industrial Society Conference that 'industry and community in this country cannot long survive with viability and future potential under the current market myth'. The notion of the supremacy of market forces is a fundamental plank of Conservative economic policy, yet the Bishop rejected it unequivocally, giving chapter and verse.

Another favourite Tory economic dogma has been the 'trickle down' effect. The argument runs that by making the rich richer, the poor will benefit ultimately through the greater spending power of the wealthy. Nonsense, according to Liverpool's two bishops, Catholic Derek Worlock and Anglican David Sheppard. In the foreword to their best-selling book, *Better Together*, they descend to the detail of the numbers of those on supplementary benefit to show that 'the incomes of the poorest groups have not kept up their share of the total disposable income of the nation'.

The bishops chose to make a specific, detailed criticism, set out not in the language of the pulpit but in that of the financial markets, with statistics provided to back up their argument. The essence of the bishops' message on this and other subjects remains that such policies are unChristian, with the word 'immoral' frequently applied to such ideas as the poll tax. They may be wrong. But the context and terminology are such as to take the argument to the government in a way that cannot simply be ignored.

David Jenkins has gone further than most of his fellow clerics to the point of labelling Mrs Thatcher's legislative initiatives 'wicked'. This remark earned him many column inches of newspaper analysis and many personal insults from Tory MPs. He describes this development in the church's contribution to national life as follows:

> The Thatcherite modification, whereby consensus has been thrown out and conviction is the thing, has in many ways carried all before it. This thrusts the church, especially the established church, though with others assisting, into the centre of not straightforward political opposition, but of speaking up for the issues that are being ignored, overridden, or for the moment settled in a way that up to now would not have been thought of as the right way.

But in doing this, the church has been only one of many voices. Other groups, parties, sectional interests have had their say on government plans. Many have attacked them with every bit as much vehemence as the church, if not more. Why is it then that the *bishops* have been given so much attention, have generated so many headlines, while others, most notably on the opposition benches, have been judged largely ineffective by the public, and duly neglected? Bishop Jenkins would suggest that there are a variety of reasons for his own, and his colleagues', enduring prominence:

> One, because England remains a very old-fashioned and traditional society which through so many changes still has a group of persons to whom it will pay attention if there is the least reason for them doing so. And among these are what you might call the leading clergy. Then there is the technical and sociological reason which is that our society is both divided and uncertain, a fact which is liable to produce in different ways what I call regressive nostalgia – people want to look back on something that is more stable, more worthwhile, and more comforting than what they've got at the moment. And if you touch a nerve in that situation, people will respond. And to that you must surely add the modern media. Whereas in the old days words only reached an elite, today when you combine the

traditional authority figure with touching a nerve, then that becomes block headlines in the papers and on television.

If we take each of these eloquently outlined propositions in turn, there is a surprising degree of agreement amongst their most vocal detractors as to the essence of bishops' press and public popularity.

Few would dispute that there exists an abiding interest in personalities and that this extends to bishops even in an age that is widely termed secular in its approach and outlook: 'Bishops are public figures and legislators in the House of Lords. They are grist to the mill of journalism and are no different in that respect to any other group,' according to one of our interviewees, Peregrine Worsthorne, then editor of the *Sunday Telegraph.*

Peter Preston, his opposite number at the *Guardian,* a paper which gives noticeably less prominence to bishops and their utterances than do its main rivals, would concur that bishops are leaders in public life as far as journalists are concerned. And as such they have a clear interest in and connection with the political debate that is at the centre of public life. There is, he feels, almost a cult that surrounds the figure of the prelates: 'I remember when I was a junior reporter in Liverpool that Cardinal Heenan [then Catholic Archbishop in the city] was such a dominant figure. Reporters couldn't fail to be impressed by the man in those mounds of scarlet.'

Clearly defined personalities – faces, names – are what the public wants rather than learned reports, findings from anonymous committees, urgings from professional bodies. And it is a need that bishops themselves share and hence recognize, as Cardinal Basil Hume, leader of the Catholic community in England and Wales, points out:

> I certainly think that people listen to persons rather than committees or councils. I have always felt that. If Archbishop Runcie speaks, that somehow gets reported in a different way than if the Synod passes a resolution. You see Archbishop Runcie's picture on the BBC news and then what he said. But if the Synod says it, you might get a picture of them filing into Church House or something, but it hasn't got the same impact. I find myself doing that. If I see 'Achbishop Runcie says ...' then I look up and listen. But if I see 'Synod says ...' then I look at it later on.

Bishops personify something more than the cut and thrust of the world of politics; they are thought to be above personal interest, and they carry that weight with them in their public interventions, as Bishop Cormac Murphy-O'Connor of the Catholic diocese of Arundel and Brighton emphasizes:

I think that people want to hear bishops speak today. In our society bishops are perceived as the only people who are really free, who can speak and have nothing to lose. You're not there by election, so they can't kick you out.

It would be a mistake to think that the attention paid to bishops' pronouncements is necessarily mirrored by the treatment given by press and public to church leaders who do not hold the title of bishop. In that most ecumenical city of Liverpool, for example, the two bishops – Derek Worlock and David Sheppard – have tried on numerous occasions to stress that they are part of a trio with the leader of the region's Free Churches. At the memorial services for the victims of the Hillsborough disaster in April 1989, the two prelates stood aside to allow Dr John Newton, Moderator of the Free Churches on Merseyside, to take a more prominent role in the proceedings in the city's Anglican cathedral, at that moment the focus of the nation's attention and grief. As Bishop Sheppard stresses:

Always we have tried and tried again to get the press to take the third part of our partnership seriously. We've actually had to put the Free Church Moderator between us to get him in on photographs of Archbishop Worlock and me. If he stands on either side of the two of us, he'll get cropped off before it is printed.

Part of the reason for this negative attitude towards those church leaders who are not accorded the title of bishop goes back to Cardinal Hume's observations about taking more notice of an archbishop than a synod. The leaders of the Free Churches take office for short periods. They do not stand above the democratic structure of their organizations in the same way as Catholic and Anglican bishops seem to dominate their churches. The moderators are part and parcel of the machinery of running their churches and their elected office carries little of the symbolism and status of a bishop.

But the reasons for the virtual eclipse of men like Dr Newton go deeper, Bishop Sheppard would argue:

> I think that the Free Churches have not trained or even expected their leaders to play a very public role. They don't give them the support staff or the resources to play that role, and in many ways it is an unfamiliar one to them. Their leaders' terms of office are short, and the tradition isn't there. There remains a certain mystique about being a bishop that in a less religious age seems to hold sway.

It is not only the media who listen to the bishops. Politicians too recognize the importance of bishops as public figures. John Gummer, an outspoken member of the Church of England's General Synod and a Cabinet Minister in Mrs Thatcher's government, is no admirer of what certain bishops have to say about his colleagues. In the past he has been particularly vocal in attacking the Bishop of Durham. Even he, however, concedes that bishops must be taken seriously by holders of public office and by the press. One reason is the size of the flock that they lead. The sum total of the congregations that fill Britain's churches each Sunday morning gives church leaders a bigger audience than most popular newspapers or television programmes can boast. Individual bishops holding forth in their cathedrals still have the attention of a crowd that any Minister would be proud to gather at a political meeting. Religion retains the power of numbers, if a diminished one.

Mr Gummer is equally at one with Bishop Jenkins on the second of his three propositions regarding the recent wave of public interest in bishops – namely that people in a changing age are looking to prelates for something more stable, more comforting. But where Dr Jenkins talks of 'regressive nostalgia', the Minister prefers to put it more positively – 'a great desire for moral values'. In his opinion, the church and the Christian faith are much more interesting, important and abiding than politics – a fact recognized by politicians and public alike.

If this need for guidance from church figures does exist, and indeed has grown in recent years as our nation has undergone radical changes, why has that same period witnessed a continuing decline in church attendance? Why do those seeking 'moral values' not pack the pews to hear in person the bishops' Sunday homilies from the pulpit?

It is only the packaging that appeals to many people. It's the ritual that comforts rather than the content. That said, you can throw away the packaging of church services and still want the contents, the essential message. The press, for one, has recognized that fact. That desire in the general populace for guidance from the church and its leaders is being acknowledged, not created, by newspapers. Tying in with Bishop Jenkins' final point regarding the role of the modern media in bringing bishops to prominence, Mr Gummer holds that the popular press in particular now legitimizes that widespread public demand for leadership from the bishops – 'for the kind of moral and spiritual leadership that people sense they haven't got'. Thus the tabloid papers only print the 'Bish Bosh' type of story they are fond of because they know that it will appeal to their readers, and hence sell more copies. According to the Minister, 'It has to be worthwhile for the *Sun* to ridicule someone. They believe that their readers have an interest in bishops being something more, something other than the newspaper is showing them to be.'

It is a point that is echoed by the Archbishop of York, Dr John Habgood:

> In a curious way the range of influence of the bishop, the range of interest in him, is not in the least circumscribed by the number of people who go and worship in churches. Around the group of consciously committed worshippers there's an enormous penumbrum of interest in the church and a lot of people expecting the church to be there as something that is an essential part of society, something that is seen to give moral leadership, to provide a sense of stability and so forth. There is a hunger for the kind of comforts which religion is supposed to provide. There's a lot of antagonism then when bishops don't say things that minister to that comfort.

But although Mr Gummer may feel that positive motives underpin the prominence given to bishops, John Habgood detects a negative trait of trying to pigeonhole prelates as rather benign figures patting society on the head, and then turning on them when they reject this role:

> There is a whole section of the press that is hostile to the churches. Their motive in reporting is usually to show Christian

spokesmen up in bad light. That may be a bit sweeping, but there is a distinct feeling that whatever you say will be taken in a way that is hostile.

Dr Habgood has a higher opinion of the quality end of the daily newspaper market. Figures like *The Times*'s long-serving donnish religious-affairs correspondent, Clifford Longley, are on the whole responsible and sympathetic in their approach to reporting religion.

Peregrine Worsthorne, when he was editor of the *Sunday Telegraph*, questioned such a clear distinction between the different sections of the press in their attitude to bishops: 'I don't recall in recent times reading a speech by a bishop that I'd want to see printed in my paper for edification. Rather we report them because we get hot under the collar when the Bishop of Durham says something that a bishop has no business saying.' In other words he feels some of that hostility that Dr Habgood identifies in the tabloids.

What is it then that the bishops have been saying to get Ministers and *Sunday Telegraph* readers, amongst others, so angry? Is it partly that anger, the hostile reaction that they have prompted in many areas of the very establishment from which they emanate, that has given them such prominence?

Dr Jenkins has explained persuasively the background to why people listen to him and his fellow clerics and there is a broad measure of agreement with his analysis. But if he was merely to mouth platitudes in his public statements or even give the generalized moral guidance Mr Gummer seeks, then there would be no reaction, no one would get upset. So it is also the substance of what the bishops say that thrusts them into the public spotlight. Their statements broadly fall into two categories: those on matters of faith, such as the Bishop of Durham's questioning of the Virgin Birth, the Resurrection and the Ascension, and those on matters which, again broadly speaking, might be called political.

In both areas they have generated anger and outrage. If the public looks to them for moral guidance in changing times, then the response of the bishops has surely been to move the goalposts and change the way that they are presenting the eternal truths of Christianity. John Gummer feels that this new approach has its roots in the 1960s:

The Church was ignored in the 1960s and 1970s by the world as a whole. 'Stuffy bishops have nothing to do with the swinging sixties' was the attitude. That was the essence of John Lennon's remark, 'we're more famous than Jesus'. The church was felt to be irrelevant and thought itself to be so. So it decided to get relevant, to shape its message to meet the needs it perceived.

The same might be said of the Conservative Party in the late 1970s and the Labour party in the late 1980s. What is wrong with getting one's message across? Well, Mr Gummer claims that the church has changed not only its approach, but also its message. The bishops disagree. They are reacting to what they see around them, they claim, to issues that are raised by changes in society. But they are still applying Christian teaching, the principles of which remain constant.

Given the numerous specific criticisms that the bishops have made of the present Conservative government, the headlines and the debates they have prompted, the next question must be how much have they actually *achieved*? How carefully has the government listened to their pleas on behalf of ordinary people? In concrete terms the answer would seem to be very little. The most often reported interventions by bishops in the political arena have been their criticisms of legislation and their urging that the government alter course. The trophies from these public confrontations are few and far between. The Bishop of Durham did not bring about a peaceful resolution to the miners' strike, despite his eloquence from the pulpit and his presence on the picket line. The Catholic Archbishop of Glasgow's description of the community charge as 'immoral' has not stopped the government on the floor of the House from implementing it in Scotland initially and now in England and Wales as well.

Labour MP Frank Field, a member of the Church of England's General Synod and a respected commentator on church affairs in several newspapers, credits the Anglican bishops with only one major victory in a head-to-head conflict with the government – over the format of the post-Falklands service in St Paul's Cathedral. The Archbishop of Canterbury stood up to Mrs Thatcher and refused to allow the event to be a celebration of victory and military achievement. With all the authority of his personal credentials as the first Archbishop of Canterbury since the Middle Ages to have fought in a war, and the only one to have won the Military Cross (for his exploits as a tank commander during the Second World War) Dr Runcie insisted that the Falklands service should remember all those who died on both sides of the battlefield. In his sermon he praised the courage of all those who fought and, to the visible discomfiture of the serried ranks of Cabinet Ministers, went on to remind the congregation in his sermon that Christ commands us to pray especially for our enemies.

There are other victories to note – principally those won in the House of Lords by the twenty-six Anglican bishops who have a seat in the Upper Chamber. Thus the government was, for example, deflected in 1985 from abolishing the Inner London Education Authority by a Lords rebellion led by the Bishop of London. It proved a temporary reprieve for the much maligned London-wide schools body. In 1988 the Bishop was not able to muster enough troops to beat off a second attack and the ILEA was scrapped. Other small concessions have been dragged out of the government on the floor of the House on social security changes and housing regulations.

But these achievements are merely the public evidence of the bishops' influence over Ministers. Lobbying by churchmen takes on other more subtle, and often more effective, forms that elude the headline writers. Given that the majority of the present government are Christians, and to different degrees practise their faith, they have a natural predisposition to listen rather more attentively to bishops than the general public is led to believe. This emerged time and again in our interviews with both politicians and bishops.

The *public* contributions by the bishops, in terms of speeches damning government initiatives, are often their last resort, when all other channels for bringing pressure to bear have failed. Hence, to judge the bishops' success rate in affecting the shaping of our society during the Thatcher years, it is not sufficient to match up issues they have made a public fuss about – poll tax, unemployment, the inner cities – and then look at how many, if any, of their suggested amendments have been put into effect by Ministers. The system by which they influence the running of our society is much more subtle than that.

Cardinal Basil Hume explained to us how this rather less public form of lobbying works:

I had a very interesting case recently when a very able woman who works at the Passage [a church-run central London hostel for the homeless] was very upset at new DHSS regulations and how they stopped people at the centre getting money. Well, I set up a meeting for her with Nick Scott [then a Minister at the DHSS before it was split up]. He came here to Archbishop's House and met the woman from the Passage, and I was present. That didn't get any press coverage but it was a very fruitful meeting.

Mr Scott may have been inspired to make small technical changes in the legislation. No one will ever know for sure. Although the Cardinal was at pains to stress that he uses this privileged position *vis-à-vis* Ministers with great care, he clearly recognized that his status as a bishop gave him an entry denied to ordinary citizens, whatever their expertise, with their elected government:

> I think it is true that if I ask to see somebody like Nick Scott then they treat us very well. I've never been refused, though I'm careful not to overplay my hand. I do get treated with enormous understanding and courtesy. I think that there is a facet in this process in which Ministers think that the spiritual life is important.

Many of the other bishops interviewed for this book had similar tales to tell of lunches, dinners, meetings set up with Ministers to put a particular case. More often than not these either passed off without the press paying much attention, or with the gathering kept on a strictly private basis.

On other occasions, however, such lobbying has taken on a more public face. Cardinal Hume led a delegation in 1988 to ask the Home Secretary, Douglas Hurd, to consider new evidence in the case of four prisoners jailed in 1975 for the Guildford pub bombings. In October 1989 the Cardinal scored a notable victory when the government's law officers announced that the convictions against the Guildford Four, as the prisoners had become known, could no longer be sustained. They were released, and one of their first public acts was to pay tribute to Cardinal Hume.

The Cardinal's involvement in this case was crucial, and symptomatic both of his personal prestige and of that of bishops in general. When he visited the Home Office he was accompanied by four other distinguished men: Merlyn Rees and Lord Jenkins of Hillhead, both former Home Secretaries, and Lords Devlin and Scarman, both retired senior judges. That these eminent figures, and indeed the whole campaign to prove the Guildford Four's innocence, should want to be led by the Cardinal is evidence of the influence that a bishop's office carries.

That was an example of the Cardinal intervening on a specific and detailed matter. In general, though, interventions by bishops tend to be more wide-ranging: delineating legitimate areas of government activity, for example, rather than getting down to the nitty-gitty of clauses in legislation. The church is one of a number of bodies that exercise such a watching brief on government activity. The churches, the opposition parties, the courts, organizations like the trade unions, the Confederation of British Industry, the media – all these to differing degrees play a part in drawing the lines of public acceptability over which Ministers are often reluctant to step.

Although it can be argued that in this policing capacity the church has spread its wings in the Thatcher years, for example embracing issues of economic policy, its essential function with regard to drawing parameters for action remains in the moral sphere. This is where bishops are at their most effective. This can be seen with reference to bishops' reports on such subjects as embryology, test-tube experimentation and the like. Working through accepted channels of responses to government consultation papers – such as submitting evidence on the moral and legal ramifications of *in vitro* fertilization to the government-appointed inquiry headed by Lady Warnock – the church has brought considerable influence to bear in an area where ethics enter most directly into the remit of the government.

Few Ministers deny that they listen most attentively to bishops on such matters – more attentively perhaps than they would when prelates choose to speak on economic questions. In such questions as the dignity of life, a senior Minister told us, the church has a distinct and historical role to play in interpreting Christian teaching for the benefit of politicians. It is when the bishops choose to speak on topics like the poll tax that the Minister listens less carefully to the churchmen's message.

There is a broader point to consider here. We have said that the majority of our senior elected politicians are Christian, so they can be forgiven for expecting a little *Christian* input to the church's considered statements on matters of national importance. The Archbishop of York, at the time of the row over the Church of England's report on the urban areas, *Faith in the City*, was reported as urging the government to take more notice of the document's *sociological* insights. He was forced to admit that the *theology* was not the document's strongest point. But as several politicians were quick to stress, the government has droves of superannuated sociologists at its disposal. Surely it is precisely the *theological* input that the church should be offering, whatever the topic on the table, for faith and the interpretation of Christian teaching is the church's distinctive contribution?

In meeting this reaction from Ministers, the Catholic church has had the same problems as the Anglicans. In submissions on such matters as abortion and embryo experiments, for example, the bishops have tried to appeal to all people of goodwill, irrespective of their faith. They have therefore eschewed arguments based on Catholic dogma, such as ensoulment, and relied instead on what they regard as the rational claims of natural law. But then their critics claim that they are neglecting their 'proper' theological concerns.

Their 1989 report on trade unionism, *A Threefold Cord*, on the other hand, has very specific points to make in criticizing Tory policy of restricting workers' rights to organize, but locates those 'political' points within the context of a detailed examination of the issue from the standpoint of Catholic moral teaching – papal encyclicals are quoted, as it were, religiously in the text. In response, the Department of Employment had to stop and take the findings of the report rather more seriously than if it had simply echoed the lobbying of disaffected trade unions. The bishops had added a new dimension to the debate, indeed they had changed the nature of the debate and perhaps even caused the Department to see some of its policies in a new light.

Such interventions on trade unionism may not make as many headlines as off-the-cuff remarks about the general immorality of government policies. It could even be argued that the bishops miss the boat by spending too long in committee getting the theology right while the issue is being settled outside on the picket lines or in the courts. But the theological element does give the church a voice of authority, one that is respected within Whitehall. And that is the crux of the matter; bishops remain men with power to make the government listen. It is a capacity they have won increasingly in recent years in a response to changing times and people's needs. Behind the headlines, the TV chat show appearances, the national personality status, there is a theological substance, a spiritual power-base, and a legitimate interest in improving this world.

Part II

Issues

———

Media coverage is not necessarily the best guide to the influence of the bishops. As we shall see in examining the work of individual bishops, many pride themselves on behind-the-scenes diplomacy. The quiet word with the Minister, the private lunch with the ambassador, the planting of a story with a friendly journalist, all these may have more impact on the real world than the widely reported controversies.

But we can usefully divide the issues which put the bishops in the news into those which are internal to the churches, those that relate to moral and religious matters in the outside world and those which lean more towards politics. The three chapters in this part take in turn those three areas of concern and will give a pointer to the sort of men needed in Canterbury and Westminster to grapple with the increasingly complex range of issues that end up on a bishop's desk.

On internal matters we begin by looking at how the two denominations, Anglican and Catholic, choose their bishops, and what this says about the calibre and credentials of today's bench of bishops. Then we take the example of the debate on a woman's place in both churches to examine how those bishops have interpreted their domestic church-orientated functions.

Of course, these are only three of many issues, but we have chosen them to reflect the kinds of concern that arise internally in the running of the churches. The importance of these issues is not confined to true believers. For example, the most secular of feminists have taken a deep interest in the way in which the bishops have grappled with the emerging equality of women. Precisely because of that fascination with religion which we have already documented, the importance of how religions cope with such issues goes beyond the confines of the faithful.

This feature is even more marked when we come to our second collection of issues, namely those moral dilemmas on which the bishops have contributed their views. For example, British public debate on such matters as abortion, homosexuality, divorce, access of teenagers to contraception without parental consent, surrogacy, experiments on human embryos, pornography, blasphemy and many more such issues are all ones on which the bishops feel entitled to make their views known. Cardinal Hume, for example, has written articles in *The Times* on matters ranging from the Warnock Report on embryo experiments to the arms race and nuclear disarmament. The modern bishop is not necessarily content to issue a pastoral letter to be read in his churches. Rather, he addresses the nation through the quality press. Have the bishops' views been predictable on these issues, have they been well put, have they been influential?

Thirdly, we have isolated a set of issues which are often felt to be in a different political sphere of action. For ourselves, we doubt whether a hard and fast distinction can be drawn between our second and third categories. Issues which are designated political always have a moral element. But for convenience we can usefully group together the bishops' reactions to debates on unemployment, inflation, discrimination, inner-city riots, Northern Ireland and education, and say that these are matters on which politicians most often resent episcopal pronouncements. Using that test, these are political matters and ones where the bishops tread warily, always conscious of the claim that they are acting beyond their remit. Of course, if they accept a traditional vision of their own role, no matters are beyond their remit. In this category, therefore, we have some of the more vigorous controversies between politicians and bishops.

The range of these activities immediately suggests that any individual bishop will have great difficulty in commenting sensibly upon the full galaxy of topics. In this part of our book we also consider the ways in which bishops are briefed and supported in their role as public commentators. It is unrealistic to expect the same person to be an expert on embryo experiments and regional variations in unemployment. So when the bishops speak on these different topics, is it really the bishops whom we are hearing or is it rather their advisers? And, if it is the latter, are these advisers organized on as professional a basis as are the advisers to the government, the opposition and other political parties? Or are the churches amateurish in their attempt to provide a moral framework for human activity, squandering their public platform by not doing sufficient homework?

4

Inside Cathedrals

———

Appointment of Anglican Bishops

The bastions of the British establishment – parliament, the judiciary, the monarchy and the Church of England – share an exaggerated sense of their own history that obscures any understanding until layers of past practice and precedent have been unpeeled. The formalities of the Church of England, particularly in its relationship with the state, have evolved over four hundred years in a way which has nearly always managed to evade too close a public scrutiny.

In their most obvious meeting-point, however, in the appointment of the bishops of the Church of England by its head, the reigning monarch, church and state have not always managed to avoid controversy. Henry VIII caused a few ripples in the pews of his nascent church when he named Thomas Cranmer as Archbishop of Canterbury. Charles I, a century later, paid rather heavily for his choice of William Laud as Primate. Laud's high-church ambitions went against the mood in the country and played their part as England exploded into a civil war that cost Charles his head.

With the coming of the Hanoverians, the naming of bishops (like much else) passed effectively to the Prime Minister. The twentieth century and its tide of secularism brought new problems. It dawned on the Church of England (rather too late, given the cases of nineteenth-century PMs like Melbourne and Disraeli) that the premier might not always be a practising member of the church over which, for all practical purposes, he or she presided in the question of appointments.

Although the wishes of senior churchmen have always guided the Prime Ministers of modern times, whatever their personal leanings in matters of faith, a demand surfaced throughout this century for formal rights of consultation for representatives of mainstream Anglicanism. These were given an irresistible boost with the establishment in 1970 of the church's own quasi-democratic decision-making body, the General Synod. Implausible as it may seem today, the rising political fortunes of Catholic Norman St John Stevas in the Conservative party and Shirley Williams on the Labour benches had raised the spectre of a 'Roman' officially choosing the leaders of the Church of England.

It was left to that most accommodating of 1970s' Prime Ministers, James Callaghan, to work out a compromise. He had to balance the clearly expressed desire of General Synod for a statutory right to be consulted, and a machinery to put that into effect, with a certain reluctance on the part of the top men in the Church of England, who saw their influence at the premier's ear being eroded. The result was the Crown Appointments Commission.

This body consists of three members of the clerical section of General Synod and three from its laity forum. On each occasion that the Commission sits, it is joined by four representatives of the diocese in question. The Archbishops of York and Canterbury are *ex officio* members, and take it in turns to chair the body depending on whether the vacancy is in the north or the south. (When it is York or Canterbury that is being discussed, slightly different arrangements obtain, but the principle remains the same.)

The real workhorses of the system are the two secretaries to the Commission – one representing the Prime Minister and the other the two Archbishops. It is this pair, described by their critics as faceless bureaucrats, who travel to the dioceses and sound out local opinion. Their very anonymity prevents many lay people from making their voices heard, however. Clerical opinions form the bulk of the received wisdom. The two secretaries then draw up a list of up to fifteen names, with dossiers on each, for the Commission to consider.

After two days of deliberations at a location that is kept secret, a consensus emerges from the Commission and two names go forward to the Prime Minister. There can be an emphasis on one or the other depending on a sufficient majority among Commission members. Again, the very secrecy that surrounds the deliberations totally excludes all lay opinion.

Since Mr Callaghan brought in this system it has been the process by which all the subsequent bishops of the Church of England have been chosen, that is to say it is responsible for thirty-five of the current forty-three bishops. Opinions on its success are varied. A review by a panel of senior church figures in 1986 gave the Commission a generalized bill of good health. However, no one would claim that it is perfect and some would see it as an institutional expression of the power of a small in-group in the Church of England, with ordinary church-goers effectively disenfranchised.

The latter view was given its most eloquent and dramatic airing in the now notorious 1988 preface to the Church of England's 'bible', *Crockford's Clerical Directory*. By tradition the foreword to this annual guidebook was anonymous and usually uncontroversial, commissioned from within the church's own bureaucracy. In 1988 such was the outcry that accompanied the publication in *Crockford's* of a stinging and bitter attack on the leaders of the Church of England, and particularly on Dr Robert Runcie, that a whispering campaign began with fingers pointed at a variety of potential authors. One of the prime suspects was an Oxford academic and clergyman, Gary Bennett, who despite his formidable intellect had been passed over for a series of appointments that he had felt himself well qualified to get.

Although Dr Bennett denied that it was his pen that had accused Dr Runcie of 'taking the line of least resistance on each issue', the secular press and particularly the tabloids hounded him to his death. His body was found in the garage of his Oxford home with his car engine running. The next day an official announcement confirmed that Dr Bennett had been the author of the piece. Days later *Crockford's* abandoned its tradition of anonymous prefaces.

Amid the recriminations that have surrounded Dr Bennett's lonely and tragic death, and the accusation and counter-accusation as to who drove him to suicide, the comprehensive nature of his attack on the leadership of the Anglican church has been lost. His basic point – and in this he was wearing his personal disappointment on his sleeve – was that Dr Runcie and the Archbishop of York, Dr John Habgood, have packed the top ranks of the Church of England with their supporters – men who shared, in his analysis, a liberal and pragmatic approach. In this 'liberal ascendancy', as Dr Bennett termed it, the two Archbishops have 'a distaste for those who are so old-fashioned as to espouse Anglo-Catholicism' or Evangelicalism – the two traditional wings of the Church of England. Those likely to be chosen as bishops, therefore, will share with the two primates a 'liberal disposition with a moderately Catholic style which is not taken to the point of having firm principles. If in addition they have a good appearance and are articulate over the media [Dr Runcie] is prepared to overlook a certain theological deficiency.'

Dr Bennett's criticism therefore was that the two leading Anglican churchmen in England have used their power on the Crown Appointments Commission to advance bishops who share with them the theological middle ground, an area that Dr Bennett had earlier in his *Crockford's* preface rejected as 'selling out' on distinctive Anglican traditions and theology.

Aside from their chairmanship of the Crown Appointments Commission, Dr Bennett suggested that the two Archbishops have other less obvious means of getting their own way over appointments. His gaze settled on the two secretaries who draw up the initial list of candidates: 'The secretaries have a privileged position. To question whether their assessments are fair or adequate is "bad form" and at once countered from the chair. It is never made clear how the list of names has been arrived at, nor how far it has previously been discussed with the Archbishops.' In other words, the two secretaries, in conjunction with the primates, hold effective sway over the names that come before the Commission.

Had Dr Bennett's been simply a voice crying in the wilderness, his comments would not have caused so much controversy, and arguably he might still have been alive – if unpromoted – today. Several senior Anglicans and at least one bishop will endorse his perceptions as to the management of their church. Frank Field, Labour MP for Birkenhead and a vocal member of General Synod, is confident in backing Dr Bennett's view that a faction around the two Archbishops dominates appointments to the 'bench' of bishops. Many able candidates have been passed over, he feels, simply because their faces did not fit the mood of the moment.

Another leading politician with a high profile in General Synod, Conservative Minister John Gummer, shares Dr Bennett's analysis of a dominant 'liberal' faction. The ten years since the Church of England claimed for itself the right to choose its bishops through the procedures of the Crown Appointments Commission have seen the elevation of men who, if they have connections with the Evangelical and Anglo-Catholic wings, share Dr Runcie's views on the 'essential questions' facing the church – the ordination of women being the principal of these:

> Historically the Church of England had a solid group of middle churchmen who were not wet about faith, but neither were they extreme about ceremonials [the Anglo-Catholic wing], nor doctrine and scripture [the Evangelicals]. However, in recent times that middle-church majority has become increasingly confused with the liberal minority. The advance of synod democracy has allowed an unrepresentative but active liberal group to wield more influence, and contribute to the current trend in appointment of bishops.

Bishop Eric Kemp of Chichester, a noted Anglo-Catholic, has been one of the few prelates openly to endorse such criticisms. He has spoken to General Synod of the undue influence of the liberal group in the church. 'It has produced a bench of bishops of very similar outlook,' he complained.

Other equally eminent Church of England figures, on the other hand, feel that Gary Bennett got it completely wrong. 'He wrote absolute nonsense. Nothing could be further from the truth,' one distinguished retired bishop told us. If anything, he added, the influence of the two Archbishops has been curtailed by the Crown Appointments Commission, as indeed the then Archbishop of Canterbury Dr Coggan had feared when Mr Callaghan ushered in the scheme.

One factor passed over by Dr Bennett was the question of suffragan or assistant bishops. These are appointed solely at the discretion of the senior bishop in the diocese. He presents the Prime Minister with two names, with an indication which to choose. When a full diocesan vacancy then occurs the suffragans are in a strong position to put themselves forward for elevation – they know what the job entails, they have proved their worth as a leader and administrator within a section of a diocese, and they have achieved a higher profile within the church than is possible for many outside candidates.

This background as 'junior' bishops also gives them an advantage when it comes to the vote of the diocesan representatives on the Crown Appointments Commission, for, as Dr Bennett remarked, the inclination of this group of electors is for someone with proven 'episcopal experience'. What he failed to realize, though, was that this trait in the diocesan decision-makers is actually halting the two Archbishops in any schemes they may have to dominate the bench of bishops, since it gives existing senior bishops a clear say in the future leaders of the church through their selections of suffragans.

The argument runs that such unusual figures as Hugh Montefiore, a convert from Judaism, would never have made it as Bishop of Birmingham had he not first been brought in from the cold as a suffragan bishop in Kingston upon Thames. And a casual perusal of recent Commission appointments would appear to bear out the view that Dr Bennett had been blinded by his personal disappointment at lack of promotion. He complained in his preface that the Anglo-Catholic wing of the Church of England, of which he was a member, has been 'virtually excluded' from episcopal office. He named Dr Graham Leonard, the Bishop of London, as the only notable exception. But he might have added the names of David Hope, the Bishop of Wakefield, or Peter Nott in Norwich, both recent Anglo-Catholic appointments, and at least six or seven others. The fact that Dr Nott, a stickler for high-church traditions, followed as Bishop of Norwich Maurice Wood, a teetotaller so low church and Evangelical that he disliked even wearing a collar, is surely evidence of just that balance in appointments that Dr Bennett was looking for, but tragically could not see.

It is true of course that the past thirty years have seen a reduction in the once all-important influence of the Anglo-Catholics on the bench of bishops – but that reflects the fact that nowadays some 70 to 80 per cent of those being ordained in the Church of England come from the low-church tradition. Hence the number of Evangelicals has quite properly risen appreciably in the ranks of the bishops. George Carey, appointed to Bath and Wells in 1987, is a typical product of the changes of the past thirty years in the Church of England. He is a former head of Clifton Theological College, the training ground for the Anglican church's most able Evangelicals.

It is this balance between the wings, reflecting the congregations in the pews, that disproves the overall drift of Dr Bennett's thesis, his critics would argue. And in specific reference to Dr Runcie and

Dr Habgood, they would suggest that rather than 'taking the line of least resistance' as Dr Bennett put it, the two leaders steer a careful course between high and low church, keeping their personal inclinations (both are thought to veer to the Anglo-Catholic side) to themselves in seeking to serve the whole church. Such a strategy of compromise is in fact not their weakness, but the very reason they have been chosen in the first place as senior leaders.

Whatever the strengths or weaknesses of the present system with regard to the two Archbishops, the role of the Prime Minister continues to be a subject for debate both within and outside the church. Mrs Thatcher's premiership has seen, as we hope to demonstrate in succeeding chapters, much criticism from the Church of England of her stewardship and the principles that underlie it. In view of the influence she has over the leadership of that church in terms of appointments, it has frequently been suggested that she has personally intervened to block candidates whose outspoken views on the Tories' failure to stem rising unemployment, homelessness and poverty she would prefer not to hear expounded from the pulpits of the nation's great cathedrals. Yet Dr Bennett, not about to spare the Prime Minister from his list of people to criticize, found her 'over-ready to co-operate with the archbishops' when the two names reach her from the Commission.

This view would not be borne out by other commentators. It is widely agreed that on one occasion, early on in her reign at 10 Downing Street, Mrs Thatcher saw fit to reverse the order of the names put forward for the diocese of London, third most senior in the church. She passed over John Habgood, then Bishop of Durham, in favour of Graham Leonard, then Bishop of Truro, whose Anglo-Catholic views conform more to her own (though the recipient of this largesse has never subsequently made it clear whether he regards women Prime Ministers with similar disdain to women priests).

Although no official confirmation of this episode exists, one senior bishop at the time reports that there was such a furore in the Church of England over the Prime Minister's presumption, with cries for disestablishment, that she learnt never to meddle again. Indeed, Frank Field would hold that although she approaches her responsibilities in naming bishops with her customary professionalism, she does not dwell on the subject too long, happy to follow the Crown Appointments Commission.

And in any case it would seem that Mrs Thatcher is batting on a bad wicket if she wants to play God in this particular sphere. When in 1987 the Bishop of Kensington, Mark Santer, was named to succeed Hugh Montefiore at Birmingham, the press was full of rumours that the Prime Minister had rejected for the post Bishop Jim Thompson of Stepney – a popular broadcaster and a man noted in his East End diocese for his commitment to the poor and under-privileged. Bishop Thompson's pastoral contributions from a major see like Birmingham would be as welcome in Downing Street as Ted Heath's thoughts on the state of the nation, or so the rumour went. Yet just weeks after his installation, Bishop Santer, supposedly the safe bet for an easy life for the Prime Minister, was lambasting the government for its appalling record on providing homes for those casualties of the economic boom forced into bed and breakfast accommodation.

The Prime Minister's one remaining area of unfettered patronage in respect of the church is in the appointment of deans – the guardians of the major cathedrals who play an important role in the machinery of the Church of England. Mrs Thatcher has only to consult the local bishop and Lambeth Palace on these posts – although as Dr Bennett, himself often mentioned as a potential Dean of St Paul's, remarked caustically, the current crop are not in general 'obviously the kind of people whom the present Prime Minister would choose'. He might, then, have welcomed the announcement that came several months after his death that a working party has been set up by the church to report on the feasibility of bringing the appointment of deans within the Crown Appointments Commission's remit.

Few in the church would praise the present system as perfect, including those who have benefited from it, but few can suggest a better way, given the position of the Church of England as the established church, with its direct tie to the monarchy. Dr Habgood himself describes it as 'the least worst method'. Reflecting on the methods employed in other areas of the world-wide Anglican com-munion, he feels that the predilection for ballots of local congrega-tions results in 'a compromise candidate elected on the eighteenth ballot or something of the kind. It is not a good way for a bishop to start.'

Given the rumours about this Prime Minister's attitude to him in regard to the London appointment in 1981, his support for the role of the premier is encouragingly Christian. 'It represents very visibly a nation's interest in Anglican bishops. The rationale behind it is that bishops are eventually going to become members of the House of Lords.' More significantly, he believes, the inclusion of the Prime Minister in the present arrangements for naming bishops 'firmly identifies the bishop as belonging to the nation as well as to the church'.

As to the possibility of a Roman Catholic Prime Minister at the apex of the whole appointments system, Dr Habgood is unperturbed. 'All sorts of odd people have chosen bishops. Disraeli for example. There's an interesting comparison with the Coptic church in Egypt where they have a similar lengthy process of consultation which leads to two names emerging. These two names are then placed on an altar in the cathedral in Cairo, and a child goes and picks one.'

David Jenkins, the Bishop of Durham, is scarcely an admirer of the present system of appointment. 'Given the way the Church of England grew like topsy, at least it does have the almost accidental advantage of quasi-randomness. But apart from history the system is inexcusable. With the pluralistic modern state on the one hand and the demands of ecumenicism within Christianity on the other, the thing is clearly wrong.'

But that weight of history that enmeshes the Church of England, as also other areas of the establishment, leaves the Bishop and other critics without a specific solution to the question of reform. Those who have benefited from the system and who thus hold power apparently have little interest in reform.

Appointment of Catholic Bishops

If the Anglican approach to the appointment of bishops can, at times, resemble the way in which chaps choose other chaps like themselves for membership of a London club, then the Catholic church's time-consuming process conjures up the image of an inefficient and flagging multi-national. The top posts – cardinals, archbishops and bishops – are filled from head office (Rome) by an all-powerful, faceless and deeply entrenched personnel department (the Congregation for Bishops), answerable only to the chairman (the Pope).

Obviously in a world-wide organization like the Catholic church there is a substantial role for the local branches to play in the process – putting forward candidates, vetoing others and advising and guiding the local representative of head office (the pro-nuncio, the Pope's personal ambassador). However, the final word rests with global HQ and its decisions are passed down to congregations in the diocese in question with the absence of warning that accompanies many a company reshuffle. Only the successful candidate and a select few know. For the rest it is a question of absorbing the news and learning to use the new, unfamiliar name with the title.

A casual glance over Britain's bishops shows that local knowledge – or even passing acquaintance – has never been too high on the Vatican's check-list for potential prelates. All priests in Britain are attached formally either to a diocese or a religious order. Of today's batch of bishops only a handful worked as priests in the dioceses they now head.

But the details of the area can soon be assimilated by an able new bishop with the help of clergy and staff at the diocesan offices – or so the thinking goes at HQ. Popularity is harder to come by. There are several in today's hierarchy, most notably one of the five senior archbishops in England and Wales, who have worked hard to achieve it, without much success. But such a failure has never bothered the Vatican. It is an oft-repeated phrase that the church is not a democracy, and this is certainly evident in an unbending refusal to transfer bishops – to a desk job at head office with its bureaucracy, for example – in the face of what is regarded as a 'little local difficulty'.

So if neither popularity nor prior knowledge of the area is required, what is? Recent years have seen a series of increasingly bitter battles in the West European and American Catholic churches over the appointment of bishops. In The Netherlands and in Austria in particular a series of appointments has changed the whole direction of the local churches against the wishes of the majority of its adherents.

The Dutch Catholic church's warm and eager acceptance of the liberalizing notions promoted at the Second Vatican Council of the 1960s about the involvement of the laity and the opening to the world and contemporary culture, has been effectively curbed by Pope John Paul II with the naming of a succession of little-known conservative-minded figures to the country's principal sees. Levels of discontent amongst Dutch Catholics at seeing their achievements of twenty years progressively dismantled at the apparent behest of Rome found their most public expression in the turbulent welcome accorded to John Paul in May 1985. Some 10,000 Catholics marched through the streets of Utrecht in a peaceful protest, while a series of representatives of the Dutch church urged the Pope to loosen the Vatican's grip. Even the then Prime Minister, Jesuit-educated Ruud Lubbers, informed the Pontiff that 'Rome seems a very long way away from here. Indeed, to be quite frank, simply the word Rome makes some people uneasy.'

The Austrian church, too, had followed a progressive line in the wake of the Second Vatican Council, with its achievements exemplified well by Cardinal Franz Koenig, the Archbishop of Vienna, an international statesman with a reputation as a bridge between East and West. When in 1987 Cardinal Koenig announced his retirement, both he and Vienna's Catholic community made it plain to Rome's representative that they wanted more of the same in terms of a leader. The Cardinal, who enjoyed a close relationship with the Pope, is thought to have advanced this view at a Vatican audience. But when the announcement of his successor came, it was of a total unknown. The new man was an obscure Benedictine monk, Hermann Groer, known only, if at all, for his sterling but unspectacular work in arranging pilgrimages to Austria's shrine to the Virgin Mary. He is not a Basil Hume and not a national leader. The Archbishop, later named a cardinal, refused to meet the press, and to this day elicits the coolest of responses from Vienna's once enthusiastic flock.

The appointment only weeks later of a priest thought to have distinct leanings towards the rather strict clericalism of the doctrinally ultra-conservative Opus Dei organization as an auxiliary bishop in Vienna only exacerbated the sense of exclusion and hurt felt by Austrian Catholics, who have simply voted with their feet, boycotting the church. In analysing the spate of unpopular appointments, one of Austria's Catholic papers stressed that it was not so much leadership qualities or local acceptability that were central to success in becoming a bishop, but rather obedience to Rome.

John Paul's pontificate has seen him addressing the problem of the unity of the world-wide Catholic communion in a number of ways – by giving a strong and unequivocal moral lead in his teachings, by travelling to far-flung corners of the globe with a regularity that would exhaust even the most robust of explorers, and by ensuring that his men on the ground, the bishops, are putting over the essentials of the faith as he sees them. Hence a potential bishop who expresses reservations about, for example, the church's outright opposition to artificial birth control, is as unwelcome to John Paul in the more traditionally minded countries of the Third World as he is in the hierarchies of the cosseted and liberal environment of Western Europe where hitherto he could have found a place.

The conflict that this policy has caused in many Western European churches has so far not been so marked in Britain. Here the ancient divisions of the islands are respected by the Vatican with a separate bishops' conference in Scotland, in England and Wales, and in Ireland. The papal pro-nuncio in London – currently a confident and assertive Italian, Archbishop Luigi Barbarito, whose charming English accent is matched only by the charming welcome he affords guests in his Victorian mansion on the edge of Wimbledon Common – deals with appointments to Scotland and England and Wales. The pro-nuncio in Dublin handles Northern Ireland.

Cardinal Basil Hume, effective head of the Catholic Church in England and Wales and, to the general public at least, in Scotland too (though technically he has no authority there), is thought to have been remarkably successful in ensuring the success of candidates he feels are well suited to the needs of the Catholic church in an increasingly secular and divided nation. The present bishops' conference contains several able young bishops (for young in terms of Catholic bishops read under fifty – as one priest pointed out to us, the Catholic church alone of multi-nationals appoints its senior men at an age when everyone else is pensioning theirs off).

When a vacancy occurs there is a formal procedure that the pro-nuncio follows. He begins by consulting the bishops 'of the province'. In England and Wales there are five provinces, based on the five archbishops: Liverpool, Birmingham, Westminster, Southwark and Cardiff. (A sixth has been hinted at, with its centre at Leeds.) If the vacancy is Westminster, a see that carries with it by tradition cardinal's status and leadership of Britain's Catholics, all bishops are formally consulted. (A cardinal's hat is the ultimate accolade the Pope can give his senior men. It carries with it the right to vote for his successor as Bishop of Róme.)

It would be an unusual pro-nuncio who would not listen to all the bishops of his country as to their preferences for the new man, if only because each national bishops' conference likes to have its balance of canon lawyers, theologians and 'pastoral' experts in the assembled ranks of the prelates.

After discussions with the bishops, the Pope's local representative will also talk to the 'consultors' in each diocese, a panel of senior clergy. In addition all priests in the diocese have a right, sometimes acknowledged formally by invitation, to express a view.

The people in the pews too are theoretically included in this broad sweep of collecting opinions. They are invited to put forward names; at least they are if their parish priest passes on this good news of their role from the pulpit. Other people have less formal, but none the less important, consultation rights – prominent Catholics among the ranks of MPs, peers and the professions for example. However, in reality the Catholic laity have as much or as little say as their Anglican counterparts. Decisions on their leaders, on the men who will guide and teach them in the troubled times ahead, are taken with only the most cursory nod to their authority.

When the pro-nuncio has collected all the opinions he considers worth listening to, he will then narrow the list down to three. Part of this paring-down process includes a bizarre secretive manoeuvre. A sealed envelope is sent to those clerics known to be close to the potential bishop. (If he is already a bishop and it is merely a question of elevation to another see, the scheme is somewhat modified.) The stark letter has been described to us by one priest as being designed to fall open with the words 'mortal sin' and 'immediate suspension' uppermost. On closer perusal the context is clear. The recipient is being asked, in strictest confidence, to give a view on a potential prelate. Confidentiality is ensured by the threat of mortal sin and immediate suspension for those tempted to blab details around the diocese.

What is more astonishing than the mode of making contact is the type of questions asked. There are approximately one hundred of them. They include: Is he a good leader? Does he give good sermons? Does his parish like him? Have you heard him speak publicly or privately against papal teaching on contraception? And, significantly, what are his views on women in the church? Once these questions have been answered to the pro-nuncio's satisfaction he presents his *terna*, or list of three, to the Congregation for Bishops in Rome. They scan the biographical details and the nuncio's research, take a global overview, and pass on their recommendations to the Pope.

With many thousands of Catholic bishops world-wide it would be naïve to imagine that the Pope spends sleepless nights over more than a handful of such appointments. Many will rest exclusively in the hands of the congregation for all practical purposes. Their preferences are clear from the Austrian and Dutch experiences described earlier. John Paul provides a broad corporate strategy of what constitutes the perfect company man, and the congregation implements the personnel policy in conjunction with the nuncio.

Quite how well the procedure works depends on your overview of the general approach the church is taking in matters of faith. If you broadly approve of the direction in which the Pope is guiding Catholicism, you will like his chosen instruments, and overlook their personal foibles. If you are of a different frame of mind doctrinally from Pope John Paul, his appointments will grate. On such pressing matters as the role of women the Vatican gives no ground in appointing its men-on-the-spot.

But it is one of the unpredictable factors in such a personnel policy that once a man is in office he can change his spots dramatically to meet the circumstances in which he finds himself, with little sanction from HQ. Archbishop Oscar Romero in San Salvador in Central America was the most famous contemporary example. He was appointed in 1977 on the advice of an ultra-conservative Catholic élite in El Salvador, who considered him a quiet man of prayer unlikely to rock the boat too much. He proceeded to be 'conscientized', as contemporary theology would term it, by the poverty, oppression and brutality he saw around him, and became a 'voice of the voiceless', a fearless and eloquent champion of the poor in El Salvador, in three years creating such discomfort for the ruling oligarchy that he was murdered as he said Mass in a hospital chapel in March 1980.

Another variable in the equation is the elevation to the rank of bishop of an outsider, a man whose direction, once in possession of the mitre, is difficult to predict, but whose personal qualities make him potentially the right man for the job, when no more obvious candidate will quite fit the bill. Abbot Basil Hume was just such a man in March 1976 when he came from his Benedictine Abbey at Ampleforth in North Yorkshire to head the Westminster arch-diocese and the Catholics of England and Wales.

The machinations that surrounded Cardinal Hume's appoint-ment captured the imagination of atheist and Catholic alike, as never before. Bookmakers did a roaring trade in predicting the potential successor to Cardinal Heenan, who had died in November 1975. National newspapers carried full-page spreads detailing the 'field' and their 'track record'.

The work of the then nuncio, Archbishop Bruno Heim, a Swiss German who had a reputation as a chef that tempted the Queen Mother to sample his soufflés, and a taste for establishment figures, was complicated by the fact that the other major see in Britain, Liverpool, was vacant simultaneously with Westminster. In addi-tion to the regular channels of advice in clerical ranks, he was not short of lay people offering him their opinion. Norman St John Stevas, then a rising star of the Conservative Party and a regular columnist in the *Catholic Herald*, lobbied publicly in his column for Hume at Westminster and Worlock at Liverpool: the eventual outcome.

Bishop Worlock of Portsmouth, as he then was, was the immedi-ate front runner. He had served three previous Cardinal Arch-bishops of Westminster as their Secretary, so knew the job inside out. He had been influential in bringing the work of the all-important Second Vatican Council, which he attended, to Britain. However, he lacked enthusiastic backers among the Catholic hier-archy and establishment, while the priests of Westminster are widely thought to have opposed him as their new leader. His popularity with the laity in Portsmouth counted for nothing. When he was appointed to Liverpool days before Abbot Hume was named to Westminster, the new Archbishop made a no doubt genuine show of delight at the challenge ahead. But he had been rejected by those he had worked with for many years for no good reason other than a question of personalities. He has never spoken publicly of his feelings at being passed over for a job that he was certainly the best equipped amongst the bishops to fill. Even within his private circle of friends in Liverpool the topic is taboo.

Another front runner was Fr Michael Hollings, whose popular spiritual writings and vibrant parish experience in some of London's poorer areas won him widespread support from progressive clergy and laity as the man to shake up the hierarchy. Again, it may well have been the attitude of his fellow priests that blocked him. For soon afterwards, Fr Hollings was poised to take over as Bishop of Portsmouth, when local clergy moved in to scotch his candidature on the grounds that he was too radical for their taste. Their influence and the eclipsing of a warm response from the diocese's laity once again demonstrates where the real power lies.

The bookies' favourite in what, for three long months, came to be described as the 'race for Westminster' was Bishop Alan Clark, then an auxiliary bishop in Northampton and now Bishop of East Anglia. His high-profile ecumenical activities were thought to be both the strength of his candidature and the reason for its failure. For however popular he may have been with other churchmen of different denominations, he roused fears amongst Catholic priests – subsequently unjustified in East Anglia – that he would carry the process of unity too far too fast. Again significantly, it was the clerics who had a telling veto. But their role was negative in the whole affair. It was Abbot Hume who had powerful and positive backers in the higher echelons of the church establishment. His background was solidly establishment and he was respected by academics and theologians. The *Catholic Herald* described him as 'the Duke's selection', referring to the Duke of Norfolk, Earl Marshal of the Kingdom and Britain's senior Catholic layman. Such support was to prove crucial in bringing in an outsider who was very much an unknown quantity to the majority of Catholics in the parishes.

Few for whom Basil Hume was then an unknown name would now dispute, over a decade later, that the Cardinal was an inspired choice. Archbishop Worlock in Liverpool, too, has stamped his mark on both that city and the course of inter-church relationships. But it is undeniable that ordinary Catholics play little role in the choice of their leaders. In fact, as we have indicated already, any too vigorous support from a section of the laity would probably have been the kiss of death to their favoured hopeful. We hope that is no longer the case. What goes on inside the cathedrals concerns all believers, not just the bishops. For the church is challenged on many fronts as it nears the Third Millennium, and bishops of sound calibre are called for if vital internal matters – most notably how to answer the demands of women within the church – are to be dealt with effectively.

Equal Rites for Women?

In 1988, the Anglican communion consecrated its first woman bishop. While all Roman Catholic bishops are male, celibate, and the majority are white, Bishop Barbara Harris of Massachusetts is female, black and divorced. Her elevation to the rank of Anglican bishop is, however, merely the most spectacular public manifestation of an issue which has bedevilled the internal structure of the churches over the last three decades and played a prominent if unacknowledged role in dictating which candidates will make it to be bishop and which will not. Successful candidates must swim with the tide of their church on whether women should be ordained as priests, let alone consecrated as bishops. Most Anglican bishops now say yes. The Catholic bishops are united in saying no.

The 1976 Vatican document on this issue explains the Catholic bishops' position in these simple terms: the priest who celebrates at the altar represents Jesus, and Jesus was a man. Feminists respond by saying that Jesus was not only male but also Jewish and a carpenter. Does that mean that all Catholic priests should be Jewish carpenters? Critics resent the way in which the church seems to ignore its origins (such as the fact that the earliest bishops, including Peter, were married) when it suits it, but relies on that history when it is convenient to do so.

It is clear that women feature prominently in the New Testament, in Christ's circle, most notably of course his mother Mary. On the other hand, the people he called to be apostles were all men. There is much debate about whether this was a tactical move, because of the social limitations of that time, or whether it was a deliberate act to give men the role of bishops. What is undoubtedly true is that the question of the proper role of women in the contemporary church is the most serious obstacle to Christian unity in the next millennium. Catholic and Anglican leaderships are poles apart on the issue. Moreover, nothing highlights the role and attitude of today's bishops with regard to the internal affairs of their churches more than their treatment of the aspirations of women members of the flock.

Historically both the Anglican and Catholic communions have excluded women from the ordained ministry although in the early Christian church, in the centuries following Jesus's resurrection, there is ample evidence of women priests. The ninth century is even reputed to have witnessed a woman pope, Joan, who admittedly did have to dress up as a man, so the legend goes, to fool the chaps into electing her to the throne of St Peter.

The second half of the twentieth century, however, has seen a decisive break with tradition in Anglican circles. Starting in Hong Kong at the height of the Second World War women were ordained to the priestly ministry. At first much was made of the one-off nature of these decisions, forced on the local church as they were by an acute shortage of male ordinands. Yet by the onset of the final decade of the century there are well over a thousand women priests in the various provinces of the Anglican communion, with the pace-setter, the Episcopal church in the United States, taking the decisive step in 1988 of consecrating Barbara Harris as suffragan bishop of Massachusetts. We anticipate the appointment of other women bishops in the early 1990s across the Anglican globe, from North America to New Zealand.

In 1971 the individual national churches that together constitute the world-wide Anglican communion decided to give retrospective approval, at a meeting of the Anglican Consultative Council in the Kenyan town of Limuru, to the ordination of women in the small diocese of Hong Kong. The Archbishop of Canterbury, then Michael Ramsey, was one of those to vote against this development, in a clear pointer to future problems for the Church of England on the issue.

Since the start of the 1970s when that breach was made officially, Anglicanism and its bishops have been in a state of nearly constant turmoil over the question of women priests, with successive Archbishops of Canterbury in particular placed in a difficult position as both titular leader of the international church, which accepts women in some areas, and the primate of the Church of England, that has so far refused to countenance such a radical break with the tradition of centuries.

The question of female ordination has split the Anglican church at both national and international levels, because its bishops have been unable or unwilling to act decisively and together on the most pressing pastoral question facing their communion. With the Anglican church at breaking point, its leaders have demonstrated neither the spirit of collegiality that binds their Catholic counterparts to each other and to a single line in matters of faith and practice, nor the cohesion around a central figure and his teaching authority that so marks out the Church of Rome.

Speaking in the broadest of terms, Bishop Mervyn Stockwood, retired Bishop of Southwark, summed up the theological composition of the anti-women lobby in his church thus:

> The opposition is a sort of Pilate–Herod grouping of the Highs and the Lows, usually of the more extreme variety. The Highs do not believe that women are eligible for sacerdotal [priestly] orders, and the Lows, while not believing in sacerdotal orders at all, take the alleged scriptural fundamentalist position that women should be obedient to men in all things, including maintaining silence in church.

Those who want no concessions for women are, in short, an unholy alliance of the two poles of the Anglican church. That division is overlaid with regional differences – for example, variations in theology and custom between the go-ahead church in the States and the more conservative, traditional provinces of Africa – and by personal prejudice. The issue of the ordination of women is so central to the identity and survival of the world-wide Anglican communion that every one of its members has a view.

The prophets of the moves towards giving women equal rights at the altar have been the Episcopalians in America. Although small in number, they have a disproportionately high profile both in the USA itself and within the international church. The first is largely a result of their upper-middle-class respectability, and the second a product of their willingness to give a forward lead to a church that needs leadership.

Some would argue that the Episcopalians are, and have habitually been, weak on theology and rather too keen on meeting the world on its terms. Others would see such a pastoral orientation as a strength. Whatever the dispute, 1974 saw the uncanonical ordination of women priests in America by three retired Episcopalian bishops who were determined to force the issue. This threw the Episcopalians into crisis. In a foretaste of the future attitudes of Anglican leaders, the bishops decided to swim with the new tide. In 1976 the Episcopalian synod, urged on by the bishops, voted by a slim majority to legalize the ordination of women. Just two years later there were 90 female ministers. Twelve years later the church had a woman bishop.

Had these American developments happened in isolation, the world-wide Anglican church might have carried on regardless. But similar moves were afoot in the Far East, New Zealand, Canada and Ireland. It is that international disparity which makes the whole debate on women so crucial. For the different provinces of the Anglican communion have in the past established a delicate *modus vivendi* which has very effectively overcome their diversity. Hence predominantly high church provinces can live alongside low-church ones. The progressives can be linked to the more conservative areas.

In this working agreement to differ but stay united as one church it has been the office of bishop that has been the focus of unity, the force bringing the world-wide communion together as one. In its bishops the Anglican Church possesses a practical working system that has united a host of differing theologies and practices. Indeed the mould-breakers, the Episcopalians in America, even go so far as to encompass this ideal in their name – their identity as a church is linked with *episcopus* – the office of the bishop.

The women-priests issue has torn that show of unity asunder, principally because the bishops within their national churches have argued vehemently on both sides of the debate, while the national primates are divided amongst themselves, and Archbishop Runcie, whose international office is essentially *primus inter pares* – first among equals – has neither the status nor the personal inclination or dynamism to give a strong lead. In any case he is said to feel in his heart that the ordination of women is simply not possible for the Church of England, his own national church. His indecision is merely storing up problems for his successor.

The division within that body has been going on for much longer than Dr Runcie's term of office. In 1963 his predecessor but one, Michael Ramsey, set up a commission to 'examine the question of women and holy orders'. The resulting report was inconclusive, as was the discussion of the subject at the 1968 international Lambeth Conference of the world-wide communion.

As we have already seen, by the time of the next Lambeth get-together a decade later, things had changed dramatically in the States, and although the 1978 meeting made no positive moves towards dealing with the issue, the General Synod of the Church of England in that year saw the debate come into the open for the first time, with Graham Leonard, then Bishop of Truro, later of London, emerging at once as the leader of the section that opposed female ordination. He told the House of Bishops in that year that:

For such a break with tradition we should expect overwhelmingly compelling reasons. Indeed I think that the question was wrongly put in the first place. We should not have been asked whether there were no fundamental objections. Rather we should have been asked to search scripture and tradition for compelling reasons for reversing the universal practice of the church for nearly two thousand years. Such reasons have not been forthcoming.

This is the kernel of the argument against the ordination of women priests – and Dr Leonard is considered to be its most eloquent exponent in the Church of England General Synod, by both his own Anglo-Catholic wing of the church and by low-church Evangelicals. In a 1986 Statement, the Bishop of London summed up his often repeated arguments against the ordination of women.

Firstly I believe it undermines and questions the way in which God himself has taught us how to speak of Him and know Him. I do not believe that it was by accident, but by God's deliberate choice, that He chose to reveal Himself in a patriarchal society and become man in Christ as a male.

Secondly the Church of England claims to have continued the ordained ministry as given by God and received from the universal Church. I do not believe it has the right or power to alter it fundamentally without destroying that claim.

Although he has lost the argument in the House of Bishops of the General Synod, as successive new appointments have seen supporters of female ordination favoured, there remains a substantial bulk of lay opinion in the Church of England's democratic machinery that remains to be convinced. No doubt they are confused by the very real disarray among the bishops, their leaders. Supporters of the measure are often little better than lukewarm in their advocacy, while opponents weaken their arguments by headline-grabbing stunts – most notably the Bishop of London's own 1986 trip to Tulsa in America to take under his wing an Episcopalian parish that had fallen out with its local bishop largely over the women-priests issue. Such an action by Dr Leonard was roundly attacked by every one of his episcopal colleagues at the November 1986 General Synod, with Dr Runcie using some of his strongest language to disown the Bishop of London's action.

Currently the debate is undecided in the Synod, although even the most fervent opponents of women's ordination concede that the prognosis is not healthy for their stance. Individual dissenting vicars have already started a trickle of resignations and applications to join the Catholic church (encouraged no doubt by that church's willingness, in exceptional circumstances, to ordain married convert clergy as priests). Elaborate plans have been laid to offer the rump of Church of England ministers who oppose women an opt-out clause and a salary for life. Time, it seems, is winning the day. Few opponents of women's ordination, surely, are considering ordination themselves. Hence, the opposition is fatally undermined in both the clergy and the bishops' section of Synod. The laity, as is so often the case in the churches, will eventually be forced to concede the wisdom of their leaders.

The 1988 Lambeth Conference, despite dire predictions of the break-up of the Anglican communion, managed to paper over the cracks, and shelve definite statements on the issue until another day, although again it was clear which way the tide was flowing. In an eloquent speech Bishop Michael Peers, Primate of the Canadian province, posed the essential question that faces his episcopal colleagues in the long run: 'Is the ordination of women as priests high enough in that hierarchy of truths [of the Anglican church] to put at risk another cherished value, unity?' The clear consensus would seem to be yes, with England reluctantly dragging its feet and falling in with the rest.

But if one price of the battle over the ordination of women has been a tarnishing of the central role of the office of bishop in the church as a focus of unity and leadership, then another has been a virtual halt in the process of ecumenism, particularly in relation to the Catholic church. One essential aspect of the talks that have been progressing between Catholic and Anglican theologians as part of the ARCIC (Anglican Roman Catholic International Commission) initiative since the *rapprochement* of the 1960s has been the question of ministry, recognition of each other's priests. Pope John Paul II has made it clear on numerous occasions that the Catholic church is implacably opposed to the ordination of women, and that it would not recognize an Anglican priesthood that included women amongst its ranks.

In language that recalls the interventions of the Bishop of London, Pope John Paul II wrote to Dr Runcie in December 1988, following the ordination of Bishop Barbara Harris by the Episcopalians in America. The Catholic church, he said, is 'firmly opposed to this development, viewing it as a break with tradition of a kind we have no competence to authorize'. Ecumenical relations would be 'seriously eroded' by the development, John Paul said. The reason that developments in the Anglican communion regarding a woman's role cause such concern in the Catholic church is not hard to discern. While Barbara Harris can achieve the office of bishop in one church, she wouldn't be allowed to be an altar server in the other.

There is a story, no doubt apocryphal, that as two bishops were leaving the landmark Second Vatican Council of the 1960s, which opened the Catholic church to the world, one turned to the other and asked if he considered it to have been a success. His colleague retorted, 'If it has been, the Pope will be bringing her husband next time.'

But the chances of a female Pope in the next century are nonexistent. Nevertheless, in the twenty-five years since the opening of the Second Vatican Council the position of women in the Catholic church has, in a similar way to the Anglican communion, become a matter of great debate. In the developed countries of the West women now hold senior administrative posts within the bureaucracies headed by bishops, they hold professorships at Catholic universities, and they demand and receive recognition of their opinions from prelates. In the developing world too, a critical shortage of priests, similar to that which first prompted the Anglican diocese of Hong Kong to ordain a woman, has seen women pushed to prominence as leaders of basic Christian communities, self-sustaining units where a celebration of belief is held without the presence of priests.

In Britain, the Catholic bishops have asked women to set an agenda for discussion. In July 1988 the Catholic bishops' conference of England and Wales announced itself ready to 'listen to the voices of women' on 'topics which seem to women to be most crucial or fundamental'. No longer for women, then, organizing the flower rota and cleaning the church. In the East London area of Westminster diocese a system of lay pastoral assistants in parishes has seen many women appointed to the right hand of the priest.

In 1980 the International Commission for English in the Liturgy issued a consultative document giving encouragement to the wider use of inclusive language in the Mass, at its simplest avoiding the term 'him' to refer to all humanity in favour of forms of words that acknowledge women's presence in the community of the faithful. Hence the 'Our Father' might now begin, 'God, lover of us all/ Most Holy One/Help us to respond to you/To create what you want for us here on earth.' Such an approach would be less alienating to women, it was argued, and would take the church back to a closer translation of Jesus's original teaching to his apostles, the first bishops, on how to pray.

Such moves and initiatives show that the Catholic bishops are taking seriously the claims of women, but are channelling them in a very different direction from their Anglican counterparts. In terms of opening up the ordained ministry to Catholic women, the Catholic hierarchy continues to resist suggestions that it could concede the minor orders of acolyte and lector – ceremonial posts whose principal duties are carrying candlesticks – to women, despite pleas from several US and Western European prelates at the 1987 synod on the laity in Rome.

In his response to that synod, Pope John Paul was quite categorical about the ban on women's ordination. 'In her participation in the life and mission of the church, a woman cannot receive the sacraments of orders, and therefore cannot fulfil the proper functions of the ministerial priesthood.'

However, in an earlier document, *The Dignity of Women* (September 1988), Pope John Paul noted the equal dignity of women with men, but stressed their 'feminine originality'. And it is this very difficult tightrope between condemning sexual discrimination in attitudes to women within the church, but at the same time, critics would say, maintaining the ultimate form of discrimination in blocking women priests, that the Catholic bishops have tried to tread. The American Catholic church has been a pace-maker on this issue. In a pastoral letter in 1988, the US bishops described a man who demonstrates 'an incapacity to deal with women as equals' as unfit to be ordained. It went on to make practical suggestions that women should be encouraged to take part in church marriage tribunals and as altar girls, and condemned the sin of sexism.

This is as far as the Catholic bishops are prepared to go in meeting women. To a great extent, Catholic feminists are content to work within such constraints, striving to develop fully their role as lay people and to reform the role of the priesthood before actually attempting an assault on the ordained ministry themselves. Pragmatism undoubtedly has something to do with it. Under the present Pope there is no hope at all of his changing his mind, or even being more flexible in his approach. But an ultimate assault is inevitable. As with the Anglicans, it would seem that the bishops are standing out against the inevitable flow of time on this question. Rather than lead, they may finally be forced to follow. The lobby for women's ordination is daily growing stronger in the US church, while in Britain the most recent statistics show that a quarter of Catholics favour women priests, with that percentage going up to almost half if we take the younger age group up to twenty-five only. Tomorrow's Catholic church will not accept today's compromises.

The bishops' current strategy of keeping the lid on the problem by conceding a greater role to women in largely administrative areas of the church is not a long-term solution. But the spectre of the disunity caused in the Anglican communion is one they cannot ignore lightly. As Cardinal Hume said to the 1987 synod on the laity, to take any steps towards women Catholic priests would be 'a development of great theological significance [that] should be undertaken only by a united Christian exploration as to the mind of Christ'. As the Anglicans have discovered to their cost, such a consensus is beyond the powers of the bishops.

5

Inside Consciences

———

Sex

God's gift to the media is the frequent spectacle of an old, celibate Catholic bishop pontificating on sex. Such gifts, it must be said, come thick and fast, like manna from heaven. The Catholic bishops seem ever ready to talk about contraception, abortion, promiscuity and Aids. The Anglican bishops, while they might know more about sex as married men, are more reluctant to exercise their teaching ministry in this context. So the media are able to portray both kinds of bishop as ludicrous figures: Catholic bishops talking about a subject of which they know nothing, Anglican bishops refusing to come down off their fences and say anything which could not be said by a secular tabloid agony aunt. Catholic bishops say 'No' to everything, Anglican bishops say, 'It all depends on what you feel would be right.'

i) Contraception

Non-believers (not to mention many believers) often cannot understand how Catholic bishops can possibly maintain their objections to contraception. Pope Paul VI's 1968 encyclical, *Humanae Vitae*, setting out this teaching, has been widely condemned but rarely read. Before we look at it and its contribution to the relationship between Catholic bishops and their laity we should note that the Commission set up by the Pope to advise him on birth control favoured, by a majority, changing the church's teaching. The Pope overrode that majority to condemn all forms of contraception except the so-called rhythm method.

According to the encyclical, 'every marriage must remain open to the transmission of life'. The unitive and procreative aspects of sexual intercourse could only be separated 'naturally'. This ruling came even though one of the central documents from the Second Vatican Council had declared that in determining the number of children in a family,

> the parents themselves should ultimately make this judgement, in the sight of God. But in their manner of acting, spouses should be aware that they cannot proceed arbitrarily. They must always be governed according to a conscience dutifully conformed to the divine law itself, and should be submissive towards the Church's teaching, which authentically interprets the law in the light of the gospel.

That passage had given some grounds for believing that change was in the air. In a footnote, it was added that

> certain questions which need further and more careful investigation have been handed over, at the command of the Supreme Pontiff, to a Commission for the Study of Population, Family and Births, in order that, after it fulfils its function, the Supreme Pontiff may pass judgement. With the doctrine of the Magisterium in this state this holy Synod does not intend to propose immediately concrete solutions.

This Commission was originally set up by Pope John XXIII in 1962 with six members including John Marshall, an English neurologist who later appears as one of the dissenting members of the British government's Warnock Committee. By the time the Commission reported, membership had risen to some sixty-four people, including the British Cardinal Heenan, who was one of the Vice-Presidents of the Commission. *The Times* reported that even the theologians on the Commission who supported the existing condemnation of artificial contraception had to admit that they could not show that this was immoral simply on the basis of natural law. They could only defend their position by reference to the authority of past teaching. The Commission's report, reflecting the majority willingness to change, said that the morality of sexual acts between spouses depended on 'the ordering of their actions in a fruitful married life, that is one that is practised with responsible, generous and prudent parenthood. It does not depend, then, on the direct fecundity of each and every sexual act. An egotistical, hedonistic and contraceptive way followed arbitrarily can never be justified.' So couples were not free to follow what has subsequently been called the 'contraceptive mentality', but they could take appropriate measures to limit the size, or plan the timing, of their family. Hence, by Trinity Sunday in 1966, Cardinal Heenan seemed to be preparing the way for change in his Pastoral Letter, read in all the churches in his archdiocese: 'Physical science has revealed new facts about nature. Medicine and psychology have made discoveries about human life itself. Although truth remains the same, our knowledge of it is always increasing. Some of our notions of right and wrong have also undergone change.'

When *Humanae Vitae* was published in 1968, therefore, Cardinal Heenan was pressed to justify its intransigence. David Frost asked him in a celebrated television interview how he would answer a couple who said they wished to practise birth control conscientiously. The Cardinal responded (ungrammatically but poignantly), 'God bless you. If they're following their conscience, then in the sight of God, which is all that matters – the priest, the bishop, the Pope doesn't matter compared with God – if every person is really dealing with Almighty God.' The apostolic delegate in London at the time, Archbishop Cardinale, is reported by Norman St John Stevas to have explained that 'God bless you' must have meant 'God help you'.

The impact of *Humanae Vitae* for Catholics is aptly put by the novelist David Lodge, who breaks off the narrative in *How Far Can You Go?* to record its announcement thus:

> In 1968, the campuses of the world rose in chain reaction revolt, Russia invaded Czechoslovakia, Robert Kennedy was assassinated, and a Civil Rights movement started campaigning in Ulster. For Roman Catholics, however, even in Ulster, the event of the year was undoubtedly the publication, on 29 July, of the Pope's long-awaited encyclical letter on birth control, *Humanae Vitae*. Its message was: No change.

The reaction of many believers echoed non-believers' scepticism about the natural quality of natural family planning. As David Lodge continues: 'There was nothing, for instance, noticeably "natural" about sticking a thermometer up your rectum every morning compared to slipping a diaphragm into your vagina at night.'

For many Catholics who had anticipated a change in the church's teaching, based on the majority Commission report, the disappointment with the encyclical led them not only to reject the church's teaching on contraception but also to reject the claims of the church in other areas. Again, this is aptly recorded by David Lodge:

> Thus contraception was the issue on which many lay Catholics first attained moral autonomy, rid themselves of supervision, and ceased to regard their religion as, in the moral sphere, an encyclopaedic rulebook in which a clear answer was to be found to every possible question of conduct . . .

In terms of believing bishops, then, the contraception issue was a turning-point manifestly opening a gap between the bishops' doctrine and their flocks' actions. Archbishop John Quinn of San Francisco, speaking at a 1980 Synod of bishops in Rome on behalf of the National Conference of American Bishops, said that contraception was posing 'a profound theological and pastoral problem for the church'. He reported that a study at Princeton University had concluded that 76.5 per cent of American Catholic women were using some form of birth control (compared with 79.9 per cent of all American women) and 94 per cent of these Catholic women were using methods condemned by the encyclical. Similarly, almost three-quarters of English Catholics saw nothing wrong in the use of artificial contraception, according to a survey conducted in preparation for the 1980 National Congress at Liverpool.

Disquiet and disregard of bishops on this subject is not confined to the 'liberal' churches of the West. The Indian bishops also asked for a new look at *Humanae Vitae* from the 1980 Synod. They requested a new pastoral statement because they had sympathy as pastors for 'the plight of those couples, many of them sincere and responsible Christians, who feel they have a genuine reason for practising birth regulation and find that natural methods are not workable in their cases for the time being'. Hence, they too thought of contraception as 'one of the most serious and critical' problems.

Perhaps the best way of linking the bishops' failure to convince their flocks as to the truth of their teaching on contraception with the whole question of the role of bishops and laity together in the universal church is to quote in its entirety a speech by Cardinal Hume at the 1980 Synod. Many bishops employ the Martin Luther

King rhetoric in which they claim to 'have a dream'. Many must have sympathized with Cardinal Hume's presumably apocryphal story, or at least with the fact that he had fallen asleep, so he claimed, during other speeches by his fellow bishops at the Synod. This was how Cardinal Hume described his dream:

> I heard a voice speaking and it spoke of the church, and I saw in my dream a vision. It was a vision of the church. I saw a fortress, strong and upstanding. Every stranger approaching seemed to those who defended it to be an enemy to be repelled: from that fortress the voices of those outside could not be heard. The soldiers within showed unquestioning obedience – and that was much to be admired: 'Theirs not to reason why, theirs but to do and die'. It seemed thus in my dream, and then I remembered, upon awakening – it was only just to do so – that dreams distort reality. They exaggerate.
>
> Then I had another vision. It was of a pilgrim, a pilgrim through history and through life. That pilgrim was the church. The pilgrim was hastening towards the vision, towards all truth. But it had not yet reached it. It limped along the road. But meanwhile there were signposts to show the way, or rather they told you that this or that road was not the right one. The pilgrim is always in search, I reflected, and that can be painful. The leaders, too, of the pilgrimage are often themselves not always clear. They must sometimes co-agonize with other pilgrims. Co-responsibility will always involve co-agonizing.
>
> The fortress was a temple, but the pilgrims lived in a tent. It is sometimes better to know the uncertainties of Abraham's tent, than to sit secure in Solomon's temple.
>
> Then I had another vision: I saw with great clarity that the insight of Paul VI in the encyclical *Humanae Vitae*, confirming the traditional teaching of the church, was surely right. But, alas, we did not know how best to speak to the people.
>
> The road-signs point the way, but signposts become weatherbeaten and new paint is needed. It takes time to get the work done. My dream became a nightmare for I saw the wrong paint being put upon the signpost, and the last state was worse than the first.
>
> We must never fail to listen to the other pilgrims. And they

need encouraging. We must speak gently, compassionately, co-agonize with them, lead them gradually and speak a language which enables them to say: 'Yes, that is right; it is now clear, we accept the teaching.' I saw the pilgrims happy because they had been led nearer to him who is all truth, and they sang their joy in praise and thanksgiving. I awoke, and said, 'Vidi, gratias.'

This moving speech made absolutely no difference to the outcome of the Synod although it clearly made the Cardinal's more open-minded colleagues think seriously about their role. Cardinal Hume's point was that Pope Paul VI's encyclical was a step towards the best understanding of human sexuality but not necessarily the last word. The church should continue its pilgrimage towards the truth. Particularly in this area of contraception, as techniques change and our understanding of the human body grows, so our understanding of the rights and wrongs of this issue may grow. Together with his pioneering, prophesying, pilgrim approach to this issue, Cardinal Hume also included a pastoral concern. He was worried about the point we have already made, that the inability of some of the previously faithful to understand or to believe their bishops on contraception led these sheep away from the flock. He wanted to gather his flock together and point them in the right general direction, rather than insist that they follow the exact path laid down by their leaders.

The reality is that his sheep are all over the place. Some believe the bishops, understand their teaching and follow it. Others believe the bishops to be mistaken but still follow their guidance. Others disbelieve the bishops and do not follow their precepts on contraception. Still others do not *understand* and do not fall into line with the church's teaching on contraception. The media, of course, would have us believe that this confusion in bishops' flocks is unusual. Yet the success or failure of the church's teaching on contraception has to be seen in the context of its teaching on other matters of conscience; for example, in relation to the bishops' preaching against violence in Northern Ireland or, more simply, any bishop's teaching against theft (for example, the sin of stealing from an employer through unauthorized use of the telephone, to take an everyday matter). On all these issues, there will be some who understand and some who do not, there will be some who follow and some who do not. Catholics have often been teased for their overpowering sense of sin, stemming from those horror stories of convent schooldays. But there is a positive side to the bishops' teaching on these matters, whether related to contraception, violence or theft. At least the bishops are making their people think seriously about the moral dilemmas that face us all in our everyday lives. As Bishop Cahal Daly told us in a different context, bishops and priests are adapting to a changed world in which they no longer have the guarantee of a superior education to that of their laity. It is no longer likely that the laity will accept episcopal teaching un-critically. This is clearly illustrated by the issue of contraception. Nevertheless, the call to inform our consciences by reference to the bishops' teaching on such matters is surely preferable to the 'any-thing goes' mentality. The bishops may have failed to convince even the majority of their followers, but they have at least made them question the values which others take for granted.

ii) Abortion

While non-believers could laugh or cry over the bishops' views on contraception but carry on regardless, they began to get angry when the bishops turned their attention to abortion. Whereas *Humanae Vitae* was concerned with how married couples should behave, but did not seek to entrench its views through the law (although some Catholic countries, like Ireland, made it extremely difficult for non-believers or non-believing 'believers' to obtain contraceptives), when it came to abortion the bishops were seemingly trying to impose their morality through the law.

Non-believers object to the Catholic bishops' views on abortion on one of two grounds: first, they might think the church is simply wrong in believing that abortion is immoral; second, they might agree on that, but think that the church is wrong to seek to enforce its views on a non-believing society through the coercion of the law.

The standard approach of the secular, non-believing world to matters of law and morals is to say with John Stuart Mill that the law should only intervene to 'prevent harm to others'. But this is far from being conclusive, or even helpful. What is harm? Who are others? The abortion debate focuses on that latter question. If foetuses, or unborn children to use the Catholic bishops' preferred terminology, count as 'others' for the purposes of Mill's dictum, then clearly the law should intervene on this approach. But that is the whole question; are foetuses to be equated with babies? It is important to stress at the beginning that Catholic bishops do not necessarily dispute Mill's approach, they might just have a different view of what counts as harm and who count as others. As the Vatican Declaration on Abortion says: 'It is true that civil law cannot expect to cover the whole field of morality or to punish all faults. No one expects it to do so. It must often tolerate what is in fact a lesser evil, in order to avoid a greater one.'

Or, as the Catholic Archbishops of Great Britain stated in their 1980 Statement on Abortion and the Right to Life, 'We do not seek to have all Catholic moral teaching imposed by law.' So why have the bishops taken a stand on abortion law? We will let the Archbishops speak for themselves:

> Our stand against abortion is one aspect of our stand against all practices that degrade human rights and dignity. Scottish bishops have made many statements, both individually and collectively, on the need to aid developing nations, on social justice at home and abroad, on unemployment problems and on help for the needy and deprived. The bishops of England and Wales issued in 1971 a major statement on moral questions which ranged over Christian living, race relations, violence and peace. Since then the bishops have tackled the housing problem, disarmament and many current social issues. The bishops have tried to defend the insulted, the despised, the disadvantaged. With other Christians we have resisted racism. We have stressed the brotherhood of man and rejected any discrimination based on colour or race. The whole of Christian social teaching can be seen as an appeal to the conscience of the relatively well-off and powerful to give practical recognition to the humanity and rights of the poor and the weak. And the social teaching proclaims as well the rights of minorities against majorities who treat them with unfair indifference or hostility ... These developing human lives may be unborn and silent but they are already our neighbours living in our midst and are part of our human family. They need to be defended ... Unborn children in Great Britain are today a legally disadvantaged

class; they are weak; they are a minority ... Law ought to uphold and embody the principles that are basic to our civilization and our existing law in every other field; innocent life is to be protected by the criminal law and public policy; no law should countenance discrimination by the strong against the weak.

This is a powerful, eloquent, reasoned statement which gives the lie to the myth that bishops simply jump from the conclusion that they don't like something to the idea that it should be banned by law. On the other hand, it will not convince those who start from a different premise, namely that the foetus is not to be treated as a fully fledged human being.

Moreover, non-believers may be sceptical of the bishops' commitment to such a gap between the law and their morality. Reading the Archbishops' statement carefully, it does not actually say that they do not *want* their teaching to be imposed by law. They may very well desire just that, but if they feel there is no chance of Parliament agreeing, it makes sense for them not to *seek* the impossible. By conceding what they cannot expect to achieve they can present themselves as models of compromise and reason which may help them at other times. And if we look carefully at the whole document, it is indeed difficult to find any principles of restraint. There only seems to be one point in the statement on abortion where the bishops do not seek to have Catholic moral teaching imposed by law and that is where the life of the mother cannot be saved without a direct abortion. Here the bishops say that Catholic teaching makes 'exceptionally high demands', perhaps involving 'heroic sacrifice', and so the bishops do not feel justified in asking the law to punish those who fail to meet such exacting standards. But the bishops tell us that such cases are 'certainly exceptionally rare or perhaps even non-existent'.

So what has this commitment meant in practice over the last twenty-five years of controversy on abortion law in the UK? As one might have expected, the Catholic bishops were at the forefront of opposition to David Steel's 1967 Abortion Act which decriminalized abortion. But the bishops were relatively inept in their opposition. They organized too late, in too amateurish a fashion, and they failed to block Steel's Bill from becoming law. When the full horror of this dawned upon them, the bishops supported various attempts to change the law, all of which have failed. In 1987 and 1988 David Alton secured a majority for his Private Member's Bill to reduce the time limit on abortions to 18 weeks, but was frustrated through what he called 'procedural mugging' by his opponents. An anti-abortion amendment to a government Bill in the 1989–90 session of Parliament holds renewed hope for Mr Alton's campaign.

Of course, the bishops realize that their opposition is fundamentally to abortion, rather than to abortion law, so that they have taken steps to encourage those facing a difficult decision not to take advantage of the legal option on abortion. As that 1980 Statement put it,

> A girl or woman should always be given the practical help she may need to carry through her pregnancy. She should be given it unstintingly and without moral censure . . . it must always be given in a way that fully respects her freedom and responsibility. Very necessary and very encouraging are the efforts of those voluntary associations in which Catholics and non-Catholics work together to attack abortion at its root, providing moral and material support to any and every mother to be who is willing to allow her baby to be born and not aborted.

This would seem an important lesson for bishops and others to learn. It is increasingly difficult for a minority of believers to impose their will through the law and it is, in any event, much better to persuade people of the merits of the moral case, to provide practical alternatives and to inform their consciences so that they voluntarily take the right path, rather than to coerce them into reluctantly following church teaching.

Nevertheless, the Catholic bishops are quite right to say that they are entitled to lobby for reform of the law on abortion. What is more, they are not alone in believing that the 1967 Abortion Act has led to abuses of human rights which Parliament ought to correct. There are many *secular* commentators who in principle are much more tolerant of abortion who nevertheless feel that the 1967 Act is being used in practice to justify the unjustifiable 'abortion on demand'.

Nor is it fair to say that the Catholic bishops are without support in other ecclesiastical circles in their stand against abortion. Contrary to popular mythology, the Anglican bishops have not abandoned unborn children. They too are deeply disturbed by the widespread practice of abortion. Hence, for example, the General Synod of the Church of England, meeting at York in 1983, passed a resolution by 256 votes to 2 as follows:

This Synod:

(a) Believes that all human life, including life developing in the womb, is created by God in His own image and is, therefore, to be nurtured, supported and protected;

(b) Views with serious concern the number and consequences of abortions performed in the United Kingdom in recent years;

(c) Commends to church members the work of those societies and agencies of the church that counsel and care for mothers and their babies;

(d) Recognizes that in situations where the continuance of a pregnancy threatens the life of the mother, termination of a pregnancy may be justified and that there must be adequate and safe provision in our society for such situations; and

(e) Reaffirms the principles expressed in its resolutions of February 1974 and July 1975 which drew attention to the need to amend the Abortion Act 1967 and urges the Government to give priority to doing so.

With this kind of support from their Anglican brethren, then, the Catholic bishops have been at the forefront of a national debate about a vital question of conscience and public policy. This time, their followers have been much more committed to supporting the church's teaching. They have not yet been successful, but as that 1980 statement from the Archbishops concluded, 'Success has so often appeared to social reformers to be beyond their reach, almost up to the moment when they attained it.' The bishops believe that in the fullness of time the rest of society will come to accept their teaching on these matters. One of the paradoxes of the bishops' beliefs on these two topics, contraception and abortion, is that non-believers claim that the church would achieve its ambition of restricting the practice of abortion if only people were better informed about the use of contraception. The bishops do not seem to be willing to bargain in this way. They have a bolder aim of transforming social attitudes towards sexual behaviour. They hope that individuals will come to a deeper understanding of, and respect for, their own and their partner's sexuality. Their success in this mission might be more easily assessed in years to come. One lesson of history, even in the twentieth century, is that one generation has seen treatment of individuals as second-class people which later generations regard as unthinkable. Blacks, Jews and women have all suffered discrimination in the twentieth century. Now, in most countries, they are regarded in their true light as of equal moral worth to other human beings. The bishops believe that future generations will treat unborn children as also of equal moral worth. Who is to say that they are wrong?

iii) Contraception again – The Gillick Saga

In 1984 and 1985, Victoria Gillick, a Roman Catholic mother of ten (as the newspapers always described her), took the Department of Health and Social Security to court over its guidance to doctors on the provision of contraceptive advice and treatment to girls under 16. The Department advised doctors that in exceptional circumstances it would not be unlawful to provide contraceptive advice and treatment even without parental consent. The guidance stressed the rarity of such occasions. But Mrs Gillick felt that there should be no such occasions at all. She challenged the legality of the Department's circular. She lost in the High Court, won in the Court of Appeal and lost 3–2 in the House of Lords. Mrs Gillick's campaign was widely portrayed in the media as a crusade by the Roman Catholic wing of the moral majority.

Yet she was critical of other Catholics, notably the bishops, whenever she sensed a lack of wholehearted support. In her autobiography, *A Mother's Tale*, Mrs Gillick describes the bishops as 'wimpish'. The implication is that the bishops should have endorsed her every legal move. But while the post-Vatican II Roman Catholic church has seen a shift by the laity away from unconditionally following the bishops in every respect, it is far from having become a church in which the bishops are expected to follow one section of the laity.

Other Roman Catholic lay people could be numbered among those who opposed Mrs Gillick's litigation. They might have taken a different view of the practical consequences of any victory by her (believing that this would lead to more teenage pregnancies and abortions), or they might have been suspicious, with one eye on the abortion debate, of allowing parental views on their children's future to be given absolute moral or legal priority.

We suspect that the bishops' advisers had told them that whatever they might like the law to have been, the law was actually in accordance with the Department of Health and Social Security's guidance, so that ultimately Mrs Gillick would lose. With that advice, it may well have seemed to them to be sensible to downplay the importance of the litigation.

The bishops did not dissociate themselves from Mrs Gillick's campaign, but they did keep more of a distance than Mrs Gillick would have liked. They expressed their traditional concern over pre-marital and under-age sexual intercourse and over contraception, but their public statements also acknowledged that the law moved in a different, although overlapping, sphere from their religious precepts.

The extent to which they could support Mrs Gillick was to take the opportunity of the ensuing public debate to reiterate their moral concerns for the welfare of their young people. Perhaps they had learned a lesson from their defeat in the saga of the 1967 Abortion Act, namely that if you argue as if the law is the central issue, then when the law is against you, you appear to have lost the moral issue also. It is a much better strategy to emphasize the distinction between the law and morals so that the church can maintain its call to moral rectitude, whatever the law might for its own practical reasons appear to condone.

By the time of the Gillick saga, then, the bishops appeared to be taking a more sophisticated view of the relationship between law and morality. Examples could be multiplied. For instance, another difficult question has arisen with the advent of Aids. Again, the bishops have clearly thought about the public policy ramifications of a social problem. The Gillick case perhaps marked a turning-point for the English bishops in their development of a coherent strategy towards matters of law and morals.

Non-Sex

In the United Kingdom, it was the publication of the Warnock Report in 1984 which focused public attention on the questions of embryo experimentation and surrogacy. The Anglican and Catholic bishops both made various submissions to the Warnock Committee. Thereafter, they both commented on the Warnock Report and contributed to the lively and prolonged debate which has now led to proposed government legislation which differs in some significant respects from the Committee's recommendations.

The Anglican bishops could be quite pleased that the Warnock Committee had adopted more or less their views on embryo experiments. On the other hand, they could be displeased by the way in which the Catholic bishops and even some secular nonbelieving philosophers condemned the Warnock/Anglican approach, which would allow experiments for up to fourteen days from conception but not thereafter, as a typical example of unprincipled, pragmatic compromising. Once again, the Anglican bishops have suffered the indignity of being ignored by serious commentators and the media alike on the assumption that their position is, in popular mythology, no position at all, or rather any position you would like.

Although this is unfair, it is true that there is far more interest in the Catholic bishops' hard-line attitude to what we might call 'non-sex'. Since the Catholic church prides itself, as its name suggests, on being a universal church, this is an opportunity to focus again on the Vatican's instruction on these issues rather than treating our national bishops in isolation.

When this long-awaited Vatican instruction was published in 1987 the Catholic bishops' official line on all these developments was made clear. The bishops were against embryo experimentation, against various techniques of *in vitro* fertilization such as surrogacy or artificial insemination by a donor, against contraception and against abortion. This is hardly news, we might have been forgiven for thinking.

Since the contents of the new instruction were so predictable, the Vatican should have been pleased that there was nevertheless tremendous interest in this statement. The secular press and public seemed to acknowledge once again that the moral high ground had been occupied by the Catholic bishops even though they did not share in or even understand the stance.

The document rightly began by stressing that 'what is technically feasible is not for that very reason morally admissible'. That is a valuable point, worth emphasizing. But then the instruction became controversial by declaring that 'the fundamental criterion' in relation to embryos is that 'the human being is to be respected and treated as a person from the moment of conception'. This ruled out experimenting (apart from therapeutic procedures), trans-species fertilization, cloning, freezing and the destruction of 'spare' embryos.

Critics would say that the instruction's rhetorical question, 'How could a human individual not be a human person?', begged the real question, which is: 'When does a human individual come into existence?' Since the young embryo can still divide into twins until some fourteen days after conception, there is perhaps a difficulty here. On the other hand, the instruction is carefully arguing that the need to respect the embryo *as* a person could be accepted whatever science discovers about the development of the early embryo. What the bishops want to stress is the need to respect the sacredness of human beings. This message is not without its difficulties, but the Catholic bishops' well-known support for the lives of the unborn has a rigour which is rarely matched by the slack arguments of their critics.

What is less convincing to non-believers is the way in which the bishops move from condemning experiments on embryos to condemning almost everything associated with *in vitro* fertilization. The following passage is indicative of what critics see as an inexplicable move from good news to bad news: 'Every human being is always to be accepted as a gift and a blessing of God. However, from the moral point of view a truly responsible procreation *vis-à-vis* the unborn child must be the fruit of marriage.'

It follows from this that the donation of sperm or egg is unacceptable to the Catholic bishops. It is condemned from a variety of angles as 'contrary to the unity of marriage, to the dignity of the spouses, to the vocation proper to parents, and to the child's right to be conceived and brought into the world in marriage and from marriage'. Similarly, surrogacy is ruled out because it 'represents an objective failure to meet the obligations of maternal love, of conjugal fidelity and of responsible motherhood; it offends the dignity of the right of the child to be conceived, carried in the womb, brought into the world and brought up by his own parents; it sets up, to the detriment of families, a division between the physical, psychological and moral elements which constitute those families'.

Again, what would critics make of this opposition to sperm, egg and womb donation? They might contest the instruction's difficult argument that

> No one, before coming into existence, can claim a subjective right to begin to exist; nevertheless, it is legitimate to affirm the right of the child to have a fully human origin through conception in conformity with the personal nature of the human being.

Some will suspect a flaw in that contention, if they can decipher it at all.

At a simpler level, non-believers often express surprise that the church does not focus more on the noble intentions of donors and the life-creating nature of their gifts. The document does say that

> The desire to have a child and the love between spouses who long to obviate a sterility which cannot be overcome in any other way constitute understandable motivations; but subjectively good intentions cannot alter the objective flaws already noted.

The biggest criticism in the secular media concerns the bishops' strictures on artificial insemination by the husband. Critics object to what they take to be the bishops' objection to 'artificial' methods, whether of contraception or procreation. But this is *not* the bishops' objection, as the new Vatican Instruction explains. It seeks to determine

> from the moral point of view the meaning and limits of artificial interventions on procreation and on the origin of human life. *These interventions are not to be rejected on the grounds that they are artificial.* As such, they bear witness to the possibilities of the art of medicine. But they must be given a moral

evaluation in reference to the dignity of the human person, who is called to realize his vocation from God to the gift of love and the gift of life. [Emphasis added.]

But that still leaves the question of why the document goes on to reject artificial insemination by a husband. We have already seen the premise that science cannot be left with the last word. Just because artificial insemination by a husband is possible does not mean it is beyond reproach.

The church's teaching on marriage and human procreation affirms the

inseparable connection, willed by God and unable to be broken by man on his own initiative, between the two meanings of the conjugal act: the unitive meaning and the procreative meaning. Indeed, by its intimate structure, the conjugal act, while most closely uniting husband and wife, capacitates them for the generation of new lives, according to laws inscribed in the very being of man and of woman.

This is a quotation from *Humanae Vitae* itself. The new instruction proceeds by saying:

Contraception deliberately deprives the conjugal act of its openness to procreation and in this way brings about a voluntary dissociation of the ends of marriage. Homologous artificial fertilization, in seeking a procreation which is not the fruit of a specific act of conjugal union, objectively effects an analogous separation between the goods and the meanings of marriage.

This argument is indeed difficult to understand. It seems to say that because sex is wrong without an openness to the transmission of life, then by analogy the transmission of life without sex is wrong. Does this really follow? Is the life-creating really to be equated with the life-frustrating?

A final twist in this area is that the Vatican does not condemn artificial insemination by the husband where 'the technical means is not a substitute for the conjugal act but serves to facilitate and to help so that the act attains its natural purpose'. This apparently means that the Vatican really prefers the GIFT (Gamete Intra-Fallopian Tube Transfer) technique which involves sexual intercourse with a

81

perforated condom to collect sperm, thus preserving the theoretical possibility of fertilization. This at least holds out the encouragement to researchers that they could satisfy the Vatican's moral criteria if they focus on the right method. It was also a 'GIFT' to cartoonists and non-believers generally who had great fun with the idea of Catholic bishops endorsing the use of perforated condoms.

What did the Vatican bishops expect the law to do about all this? Some attention has been accorded the injunction to engage in 'passive resistance' where necessary, although perhaps one should read this as a condemnation of *violent* resistance such as the bombing of clinics. The instruction maintains the bishops' acceptance that the civil law must sometimes tolerate, for the sake of the public order, things which it cannot prohibit without a greater evil resulting. But rights must be recognized and respected. The law ought to forbid experimentation on embryos. It should not legalize third-party involvement. But the instruction is quite explicit in saying that believers must not merely seek to change the law, they should also seek to secure and consolidate 'the widest possible consensus' in support of the instruction's precepts.

Needless to say, this global statement was not the last word on non-sex from the bishops. For example, a 1988 report on yet another surrogacy saga in Italy raised again the question of the bishops' response to the problems posed by infertility. A 39-year-old Roman mother of three wanted a fourth child by her second husband. But she was warned that another pregnancy might be dangerous. Her 20-year-old daughter by her first husband agreed to act as the surrogate mother, offering her womb to bring to term the baby who is genetically linked to her mother and step-father. The church spoke out against what its priests described as a 'serious eclipse' of moral values.

This is only yet another variation on a very old theme. Contrary to popular opinion, the first surrogate baby was not Baby M in the USA nor Baby Cotton here but Baby Ishmael in the Book of Genesis. Abraham and Sarah, believing mistakenly that Sarah was infertile, used their slave-girl Hagar as a surrogate mother. The three parents endured all the contemporary problems of jealousy between the surrogate and commissioning mother and of conflicting feelings as to who should keep the child. Most importantly, of course, we should be concerned about and feel sorry for Ishmael, the child. Yet for all those problems, at least Ishmael was alive. And this is where outsiders find the Catholic bishops' attitude to surrogacy strange.

The child may suffer torn loyalties or a sense of displacement. But without surrogacy that child would never have existed. Should not a pro-life church rejoice at the possibilities of new life? Should not a pro-parenthood church praise surrogates for what is often, as in the Italian case, a selfless gift to someone who wants to be a mother to another child but cannot physically achieve that noble aim without help?

No, according to the bishops. The church has its own reasons for opposing surrogacy. This was highlighted not only by the Vatican instruction but also by the British Bishops' Joint Committee on Bio-Ethical Issues *Response to the Warnock Report*. Although the Committee endorsed the report's conclusions on surrogacy (not all of which, incidentally, have been accepted by the government), it felt that the Warnock Committee had focused on the wrong arguments:

> Surrogacy does indeed violate human dignity. But it does so, fundamentally, for a reason which the Inquiry does not recognize: the proper context of human procreation is that exclusive sexual union which is called marriage, in which human affection, and exclusive and open-ended commitment, and the transmission of the bodily life of the partners, form the context in which the child is helped to find and form his own identity. Deliberate rupturing of that context does indeed treat bodily life and capacities immorally.

That is an exacting doctrine, too exacting perhaps to form the policy for the law in a pluralist society where others feel that the gift of life is such a wonderful way of affirming a childless marriage that the law should not penalize those who engage in surrogacy for love rather than money. That feeling does indeed look like forming the basis for the law in the United Kingdom. The Surrogacy Arrangements Act 1985 was the only legislative response to the Warnock Report in the first five years after its publication. That statute has outlawed commercial agencies, one of the few Warnock recommendations on which there seemed to be widespread agreement. But the White Paper, issued in preparation for the legislation due to be introduced in the 1989–90 parliamentary session, suggests that the government is not keen to extend the prohibitions on surrogacy to non-commercial arrangements, adopting in effect the Warnock dissenting view.

This does not seem to be an unreasonable way forward for the law. But what is the most reasonable way forward for the bishops in their response to issues like the Italian surrogacy case? There are, perhaps, two ways in which the bishops can give a lead in dragging media attention away from the sensationalism of its surrogacy coverage and directing society's concern to more pressing matters.

First, the British bishops' response to the Warnock Report made the best point in the whole debate when it noted the report's 'striking silence about the causes of infertility, and its consequent failure to consider how social policy might seek to reduce infertility by attending to its causes'. The bishops should build on this foundation by calling for (and perhaps even funding) more research into the causes of infertility and how to prevent them. Not all infertility is avoidable, of course, but there should be more effort made in this direction.

Second, the bishops should continue to locate the debate about surrogacy within the wider debate about the family, the duties of parents and the rights of children. Those who are fertile also have dilemmas about parenthood. Should they, for example, leave their children with nannies or child-minders? This is a topic which has preoccupied the popular press recently with respect to royalty. But it is a matter of concern also to those parents who feel they cannot afford not to continue working after their children are born. Are surrogates just ante-natal nannies? Are children caused more problems by having several surrogate parents after birth rather than before birth? These are not easy issues to resolve, but they have more relevance to most lives than do isolated cases of surrogacy. The bishops are well placed to lead the debate about family life in the right direction and add their own distinctive contribution. This does not mean a call for *legislation* to save the family. It indicates, rather, a need for *education* to enable us to take morally informed decisions for ourselves and our children.

If we had to fault the bishops for their contribution to the broader debate about test-tube babies, it would be on the ground that they have not spoken in a language which ordinary people can understand. Words like 'homologous' are of no use whatsoever in persuading the average person in the pew to believe in the bishops' teaching. This, therefore, is the next challenge awaiting bishops who seek to inform our consciences. They must learn to translate the technical jargon of the moral theologian into everyday language. Although he did not have to grapple with the advances of modern bio-technology, Christ spoke in a way which his listeners could comprehend. His successors should do the same.

Blasphemy

We have so far focused on the Catholic bishops and their attitudes to sex and non-sex. It may come as a surprise to some critics of the bishops, but there are many other matters of conscience beyond those relating to sex. We have chosen as our final example in this chapter a different kind of topic which has preoccupied the Anglican bishops. Blasphemy seems a suitable question of conscience for the Anglican bishops because they clearly feel uneasy about their privileged position as the established Church of England. In a multi-cultural society, it is an important question for believers and their bishops as to how much respect they should give to other believers (e.g. Muslims), and to what extent they should expect non-believers to respect their beliefs. The reason for media interest in the bishops' views on this topic is not solely the Salman Rushdie affair. That saga must be put in context. The Anglican bishops had been thinking about the law on blasphemy well before Rushdie's book, *The Satanic Verses*, was published. The issue of blasphemy is perennial. Indeed, all religions begin by being condemned as blasphemous.

What was described in 1988, for instance, in letters to *The Times* as 'obscene' and 'most offensive' and to the *Guardian* as 'outrageous ... quite offensive ... peculiarly insensitive ... dangerous'? These are the terms which sprang to many Christian minds a decade earlier when *Gay News* published a poem and a picture depicting Christ as a homosexual, which led Mary Whitehouse to instigate a successful private prosecution (the first for fifty years). But on this occasion they were being used by non-Christians to describe a postmark authorized by the Post Office for franking the mail throughout Lent: 'Jesus is alive'. This gave rise to the glorious headline 'When Franking Incenses' under which Bernard Levin argued in *The Times* for a sense of proportion and tolerance. The Director of Development at the British Humanist Association had complained in his letter to the *Guardian* that 'those of us who believe that Jesus is dead – and have devoted some thought to the matter – do not wish to be told every day for six weeks that he isn't'. Mr Levin suggested that people who think like that should just throw away the envelopes, perhaps even mastering the skill of opening them with their eyes shut so as to avoid the message.

Many Christians will agree. But some of them are not content with being told to adopt the same approach to *Gay News*, namely throwing its blasphemous poem into the wastepaper bin or better still not buying the paper in the first place. Indeed, *Gay News* is less intrusive since it is not deposited through our letterboxes against our wills. On the other hand, many will feel that *Gay News* is wrong and the Post Office right, that they are justified in feeling offended, whereas the anti-frankers are being hyper-sensitive (and to the truth). We have reached, in other words, a classic dilemma for a liberal, pluralistic democracy. To what extent should the law protect our beliefs from ridicule? How should we balance our commitment to our own faith with a respect for the consciences and sensitivities of those who have other faiths or no faith at all?

Enter the Anglican bishops who had just recommended changes in the law against blasphemy. The matter had been considered by a group under the chairmanship of the Bishop of London, and their report had been forwarded by the Archbishop of Canterbury to the Lord Chancellor. Dr Runcie had himself 'considered the Bishop's new report with care' and 'was happy to identify myself with its reasoning and conclusions'.

The report recommended that Parliament should enact law to reflect the views of the minority who dissented from the Law Commission Report on Blasphemy published in 1985. The existing common law offences should be abolished and replaced by a new statutory offence protecting *all* religions. This would penalize anyone who published grossly abusive or insulting material relating to a religion with the purpose of outraging religious feelings. The majority on the Law Commission (which had unusually split 3–2 on this issue) had recommended that the old offences be abolished but not replaced at all.

The Law Commission's report was preceded by a working paper in 1981 which had attracted an 'exceptionally heavy response'. Of the 1,800 contributions, over 1,700 wanted to retain an offence of blasphemy in some form or other. Tracing events back still further, we find that the real impetus for considering reform of the law came with the *Gay News* case. The newspaper had not only published a poem and picture depicting Christ as a promiscuous homosexual, but portrayed in explicit detail homosexual acts with the body of Christ immediately after his death. The editor and publishers were convicted of blasphemous libel for 'vilifying Christ in His life and in His crucifixion'.

The question for the Law Lords was whether the crime of blasphemous libel required an intention to produce shock and resentment among Christians or whether the crime could be committed by merely intending to publish a poem which in practice had that effect, even if the publisher did not mean to upset others. Two judges decided one way, two the other.

The result therefore hinged on the views of the fifth, final and most junior Law Lord at the time, Lord Scarman. He has the reputation of being the most liberal of British judges. He tends to escape criticism from the left, who accuse other judges of being conservative. Which way would he decide? For *Gay News*? No, he joined Lords Dilhorne and Russell in rejecting *Gay News*'s arguments and concluding that the prosecution did not have to prove the specific intention of causing offence. But, for our purposes, what is most intriguing is the opening passage of his judgement:

> My Lords, I do not subscribe to the view that the common law offence of blasphemous libel serves no useful purpose in the modern law. On the contrary, I think there is a case for legislation extending it to protect the religious beliefs and feelings of non-Christians. The offence belongs to a group of criminal offences designed to safeguard the internal tranquillity of the kingdom. In an increasingly plural society such as that of modern Britain, it is necessary not only to respect the differing religious beliefs, feelings and practices of all but also to protect them from scurrility, vilification, ridicule and contempt.

That idea of broadening the ambit of the law is essentially the position adopted by the Church of England. Lord Scarman's judgement had set the wheels of law reform in action. The Law Commission stated that this part of the law was unacceptably uncertain, that the majority Law Lords' conclusions on intention were unsatisfactory and that the limitation of the offence to the protection of the Christian religion was, in the circumstances now prevailing in England and Wales, unjustifiable. The Bishop of London's group endorsed all those sentiments. But two conclusions could follow: abolish the offence without replacement, or abolish the offence and substitute a new offence which is in one sense narrower (requiring proof of a specific intention to outrage the feelings of others) but in another sense broader (applying to all religions). The majority Law Commissioners preferred the former option. The Bishop's group took the latter path in the footsteps of the Law Commission minority.

The Bishop of London's report rightly criticized the Law Commission for ignoring freedom of religion. The Bishop's group observed that the UN's Universal Declaration of Human Rights and the European Convention on Human Rights recognize not only freedom of expression, on which the Law Commission concentrated, but also freedom of religion as a fundamental human right.

Of course, the Bishop's report has its limitations. Ignorance of the law is not an excuse which carries much conviction when the bishops choose to make recommendations about law reform. Yet, for example, there is no mention of the fact that the *Gay News* case was itself taken to the European Commission on Human Rights. The conclusion there would have supported the Bishop's group since the European Commission felt there was no doubt that *Gay News*'s freedom of expression was limited by other people's freedom of religion and rejected the editor's claims as manifestly ill-founded. The Bishop's group's patchy legal knowledge did not extend to this important decision under the European Convention. More important, the report failed to locate the blasphemy question accurately within the wider debate about when the law should intervene to protect groups from being offended (the John Stuart Mill debate we have already mentioned, which encompasses racism, pornography, the use or abuse of sex, violence and abusive language on television and much more besides).

But the report did amount to a useful survey of some of the practical problems involved in reforming the law on blasphemy. Once it is proposed to widen the protection afforded the law beyond the Church of England, how is religion to be defined for these purposes? The Bishop's group considered four possibilities: defining 'religion' in general terms, using the term without definition, listing the major religions with a power to add to the list by order, defining religion by reference to religious groups having places of worship certified under the Places of Worship Registration Act 1855. They opted for the second course of action, or perhaps inaction, observing that the international documents already mentioned do not define the term and that the Indian Penal Code has operated for more than a century with an offence in general terms under which the deliberate wounding or outraging of the religious feelings of any person is prohibited. The group acknowledged that the adherents of some faiths which we generally regard as religions would not themselves accept that they are religions. The terms hinduism and buddhism, for example, are collective descriptions of groupings of beliefs, with at least one variety of hinduism verging on the atheistic. But the group expected adherents of these beliefs to come within the protection of the proposed law. The beliefs which the group envisages receiving the law's protection are perhaps indicated by another appendix which also has the merit of listing the 1980 statistics for religious adherents in the UK: Church of England 9,628,000; Catholic 3,182,000; Methodist 651,139; United Reformed 222,049; Baptist 210,646; Jews 466,000; Muslims 830,000; Hindus 380,000; Sikhs 210,000; Buddhists 121,000.

The Bishop of London's group placed great weight on the symbolic importance of the law:

It is often not so much what the law specifically says as the general underlying attitudes and values which it is held to express that are of importance for social well-being . . . Feelings for the sacred should not be undermined . . . We feel that the public debasement of Christian imagery, besides being deeply offensive to many Christians, may lead to a blindness to the things of the spirit and be seen as a corruption of the mind with regard to what we believe to be the most important features of human life.

The report argued that the same respect for religious sensibilities should be extended to other beliefs, the proposed law thus forming

> a cohesive and supportive element in the plural society of the country today ... It is about the manner and the extent to which a person's deepest feelings about matters of the greatest concern are truly accepted within the community by being given the protection of the law.

This report is, therefore, a prime example of the Anglican bishops working to provide answers to fundamental questions not only about law and morals, but also about the balance between tolerance and commitment in a pluralistic society. Of course, we again return to the point that the bishops' concerns transcend law reforms and that their expertise does not lie predominantly in the law. So perhaps the most important point for the Anglican bishops to make would be to place the onus on each of us to examine our own attitudes and practices, to urge us to recognize and implement 'the duty of all citizens, in our society of different races and of people of different faiths and of no faith, not purposely to insult or outrage the religious feelings of others'. It was, in fact, the minority Law Commissioners who said that, but the Bishop's report also endorses those sentiments.

The majority Law Commissioners, writing in the mid-1980s, clearly assumed that the publication or distribution of blasphemous material was not likely to lead to public disorder. Indeed, they said as much. How wrong they were. Towards the end of 1988 and at the beginning of 1989, there were scenes of public disorder in England in reaction to Salman Rushdie's book *The Satanic Verses*, which Islamic believers interpreted as being blasphemous in its treatment of their Prophet. Since the British law was assumed not to extend to cover non-Christian beliefs, outraged believers took to the streets and burnt copies of the book. Elsewhere in the world, particularly in Pakistan and Iran, there were widespread disturbances. Blasphemy became a major international issue. The topic moved away from the realm of this chapter, a question for the conscience of individual writers, and into the world of the next chapter, affecting international relations and national politics. As is well known, the Ayatollah Khomeini declared Rushdie to be an apostate and sentenced him to death. Freedom of speech, of a writer's imagination, seemed to be clashing with freedom of religion, or at least the freedom of religious groups not to have their beliefs challenged in what they felt was a scurrilous way. Where did the Anglican, and for that matter Catholic, bishops stand on this issue?

The British media, of course, expected to find the Anglican bishops sitting on the nearest available fence with their gaitered legs dangling on either side. On the one hand, Salman Rushdie was a naughty boy, on the other hand, so was the Ayatollah. This raises a wider question about believing bishops. Do they really believe that their faith is the one true faith? Or is it just one item on a menu, from which one could equally satisfactorily select an Islamic offering? The legendary wishy-washiness of Anglican bishops was contrasted with the legendary commitment (some would say inflexibility or intolerance) of the Ayatollah.

In fact, however, the Anglican Bishop of Bradford had grappled with these issues to great effect. As bishop to the area in which *The Satanic Verses* was first burnt, in which the large Muslim community was particularly vigorous in its opposition to Rushdie's book, he did *not* sit on any fences. First, Bishop Robert Williamson asked Salman Rushdie's publishers to reconsider the distribution of the book. Then he asked his own flock, the wider community in Bradford and the rest of the country to take Muslim objections seriously. He matched his words with actions, bringing together different community leaders in Bradford.

Eventually, however, he felt that Muslim protests were going too far. By the middle of June 1989, anti-Rushdie protests in Bradford were degenerating into violence. On one occasion, several hundred anti-Rushdie protestors rampaged through Bradford's centre with the result that fifty or so were charged to appear before magistrates. The Anglican Bishop of Bradford held talks with the local chairman of the Council for Mosques, Mr Sher Azam, and the Assistant Chief Constable of West Yorkshire. He warned Muslim leaders that there was 'rising anger and fear' in Bradford, such that continuing protests of that nature might deafen people to the Muslims' genuine feelings of outrage over the publication of the novel. He called on the Muslim community to ask the fundamental question as to whether such behaviour was an appropriate way to demonstrate its legitimate concerns over Rushdie's book. 'There is a real chance', he said, 'that these protests may be counterproductive and serve only to isolate the Muslim community.'

Bishop Williamson, therefore, was certainly not guilty of failing to guide consciences. He had asked Salman Rushdie and Viking Penguin to examine their consciences, he had initially stressed that outraged Muslim reaction was understandable and conscionable but he had ultimately also asked Muslims to accept that they should not in conscience risk an escalation to violence. Needless to say, he had also vigorously condemned the Ayatollah's death threats to Rushdie.

This is the way in which bishops should respond to contemporary problems. Of course, their advice is not always going to be heeded, especially by those who do not consider themselves to be part of the Bishop's flock. Mr Sher Azam, for instance, said that, while he appreciated the Bishop's concern, Bishop Williamson 'does not fully recognize what it is like for a minority with no privileges or position of power which the majority take for granted'. How true. No one can dispute the fact that the Church of England has privileges and power. Many think that it would do well to give up its established position, although others feel that such a move would diminish its power to a point which would imperil its ability to influence our lives positively. But Bishop Williamson did at least try to bring the communities together, as a reconciler or pastor. His example, of action on the ground, is worth a dozen abstract reports. If we are to believe bishops when they seek to inform our consciences, they must show us that informed consciences lead to more Christ-like behaviour. They can only do that through the witness of their lives.

But that is why this is such a difficult topic for the bishops. What would Christ have done over the blasphemy issue in general or the Rushdie saga in particular? One crucial point which the Anglican bishops, but not all their followers, seem to appreciate is that Christ was himself executed for blasphemy. Christ's willingness to forego his legal or even moral rights, to turn the other cheek, to go the extra mile, would point in the direction of a restrained approach to those who insult religious believers.

Another vital aspect of the Rushdie saga is to recall the special concern Christ showed for those who were marginalized or disadvantaged in society, for minorities: 'Inasmuch as you have done it unto one of the least of these my brethren, you have done it unto me' (Matthew 25, 21). So, Christ-like behaviour in the aftermath of the publication of *The Satanic Verses* would surely have been, on the one hand, slow to invoke legal remedies but, on the other hand, quick to comfort those Muslims who felt that the book was an attack on *them*.

This is a central distinction for the law to confront. Christ and, we suspect, an increasing number of his bishops, might well take the line that God can look after himself. The law against blasphemy is not needed to protect God, at least from the perspective of the Christian tradition, although Islamic faith may dictate otherwise. But an attack on people's faith is often perceived by them, however mistakenly, as an attack on the *members* of that community of believers. In other words, beneath the rhetoric of indignation claiming that *The Satanic Verses* insulted the Prophet and above all Allah, there is an underlying fear amongst many members of the Muslim community in the United Kingdom that Rushdie's book harmed them. It could have encouraged a line of 'reasoning' that runs: if anyone could follow such a prophet, they must be strange folk. At this point Christ and his bishops might well feel that steps have to be taken to reassure what is, in the United Kingdom, still a minority community. Their contribution to British society needs to be valued, their faith needs to be respected. They need to be reassured that their fellow citizens (not to mention Rushdie himself) would certainly not want them to feel diminished by anything which *The Satanic Verses* might have to say about Islam.

But, as the Bishop of Bradford found, Muslims *did* feel diminished by the book. To them, it did not matter that they might not have read it. It did not matter that Rushdie was writing on a clever plane. The book upset them and they wanted something done about it. The secular, white media did not pay attention until the book-burning and particularly the Ayatollah's death threat.

In many ways, the Anglican bishops were the most unlikely saviours of the Muslim community, in other ways the most predictable. They were unlikely because, as the Bishop of London's report suggested, the Anglican bishops had a particular difficulty in participating in rational constructive debate about the law on blasphemy. Their problem was (and is) that they have been given special privileges by the law as an established church. In the modern era, they do not wish particularly to be given such preferential treatment. It embarrasses them. On the other hand, if they forego their privileges and argue against any law of blasphemy at all, that will be interpreted by their critics as yet another sign of the secularization of the Church of England. So their first instinct, pre-dating the Rushdie affair, was to extend the law on blasphemy so as to bring other faiths within its protection. But, a law on blasphemy designed (unnecessarily) to protect God fits uneasily, if at all, with the rest of the law. Restrictions on free speech should only be tolerated where necessary, for example in relation to genuine and pressing claims of security. So the Bishop of London's position of extending the blasphemy law was unlikely to survive the Rushdie affair. The bishops should instead have been seeking to shift the focus of attention from the worry that Rushdie was offending God to the worry that he was denigrating the members of religious/ethnic minorities. This might have led to arguing for an extension of the incitement to racial hatred law so as to encompass incitement to religious hatred (which is already prohibited by law in Northern Ireland, although no successful prosecutions have been conducted). We should stress that we believe that Rushdie would have been innocent of any such intent or charge. Our point is that the debate should have been on those terms.

In many ways the Anglican bishops were exactly the kind of cavalry you would expect to ride to the rescue of the apparently beleaguered Muslims. The Anglican bishops are caricatured in some parts of the British media as ready to jump on to any bandwagon, any mood of the moment or, because of their time-lag in understanding modern trends, any mood of yesterday. Dr Runcie's September 1989 sermon in Canterbury Cathedral, which seemed to announce that God is now Green, would be one example. The excessive tolerance, in the eyes of some critics, of Islam would be another.

Hence it came as no surprise, in July 1989, when the media revealed that the Archbishops of Canterbury and York were having meetings with representatives of the Muslim community and trying to find a creative solution to the Rushdie problem. Although the bishops had done the right thing in commissioning the earlier report, its limitations were by now evident, and it was set to be discarded. Similarly, the government seemed to appreciate the limitations of the Law Commission majority and minority reports. The majority report seemed impractical, given that it would put nothing in place of the law on blasphemy. It had also miscalculated the trouble that could be caused by blasphemy. The minority report, on the other hand, would seem only to compound all the problems of concentrating too many minds on too many blasphemies. Critics on all sides attacked the government and the Anglican bishops. Some wanted an extension of the law. Many wanted its complete abolition. With those behind crying forward and those in front crying back, the government tried to stand its untenable ground by maintaining the existing imperfect law. The Archbishops, in contrast, set up a small working party with Muslim leaders, charged with the task of producing more creative ways forward.

Whether or not the bishops can produce answers to what seems to be an intractable problem, these gestures are in themselves valuable, however denigrated they might be by commentators. The fact that the bishops seemed much happier in the company of leaders of other faiths than with politicians or journalists is itself highly significant. Critics expect bishops to tell leaders of other faiths that they are wrong and to urge their own followers to new vigour and rigour in their one, true faith. Yet the Archbishop of Canterbury and other bishops seem to do the exact opposite. Dr Runcie criticized fundamentalists within his own church in no uncertain terms during the course of 1989, while he seemed to go out of his way to tolerate intolerant Islamic fundamentalists. Why? Our own impression is that the bishops enjoy the company of devoutly religious people of whatever faith. They cherish the ethnic and religious minority communities in the United Kingdom precisely because such groups hold religious values so dear. The secularist society which we are alleged to live in has, since the 1960s, trumpeted a different set of anti-religious values. It is, in fact, the secular commentators who have failed to keep up with the times and the Anglican bishops who are (some would add, for once) thinking ahead. The chattering classes have long convinced themselves that God is dead, at least in Hampstead. They have waffled on about the problems of 'racial' minorities, ignoring the fact that such minorities often see themselves as *religious* communities. God is alive and well and certainly living in Bradford. The bishops, and many others, believe this. The Rushdie saga made them stop and think: what implications does belief have for their own faiths, their own moral consciences, the law and politics? As second-rate lawyers and third-rate politicians, the bishops cannot be expected to have all the answers. But in their Christ-like concern, in the witness of their own reaction to the issues, they have provided an example to all believers.

6

Outside Politics?

_____

While everyone believes the bishops have the right to govern within their own cathedrals (although some would like more democracy), and most people believe that the bishops have the right to teach on matters of conscience, there is much greater disagreement as to the legitimacy of episcopal involvement in politics.

According to the Second Vatican Council, the Catholic church 'has the right to pass moral judgement, even on matters touching the political order, whenever basic personal rights or the salvation of souls make such judgements necessary'. But there are tensions here. The present Pope has been compared to T. S. Eliot's Becket, as, when Cardinal Archbishop of Krakow, he was involved in a political relationship with the leaders of Poland, which is, despite three decades of Communist government, clearly a Catholic country. Yet the same man, as Pope John Paul, ordered Father Drinan, an American Jesuit, to give up his seat in Congress and ordered priests in the Sandinista government in Nicaragua to give up their ministerial offices. Father Drinan agreed, but the Nicaraguan minister–priests rejected the Pope's instructions and were suspended from their active ministry. In both cases, the Pope wanted his clergy to leave party politics to the laity. The ruling is now enshrined in the revised Code of Canon Law promulgated by the Pope.

The Second Vatican Council put this point well in the document *Gaudium et Spes*, where we are told: 'Let the layman not imagine that his pastors are always such experts, that to every problem which arises, however complicated, they can readily give him a concrete solution or even that such is their mission.' And Pope Paul VI reiterated the point in his 1971 *Call to Action*: 'In concrete situations, and taking account of solidarity in each person's life, one

97

must recognize a legitimate variety of possible options. The same Christian faith can lead to different commitments.'

Yet the laity, and certainly the religious and secular press, still seem to expect words of wisdom from the bishops on almost every political and legal issue. In one week in 1986, for example, *The Times* interviewed Cardinal Hume about the government's attempts through advertisements to prevent the spread of Aids, while the Cardinal himself wrote to *The Times* about the miscarriage of justice in the case of the Guildford Four. Simultaneously, the *Catholic Herald* reported that the bishops had just devoted a meeting to discussion of the law and morality of Sunday horse-racing! So where does the bishops' expertise and authority stop? And when, if ever, does the hierarchy consciously choose to refrain from public pronouncement, feeling that an issue is more suitable for the gifts of the laity to resolve?

When the Catholic bishops issued a statement in support of a Bill of Rights in the same year, for example, we might have been forgiven for wondering whether their opinion, however well-intentioned, was especially valuable. We can be for human rights but hesitant about a Bill of Rights. An entrenched Bill of Rights shifts power away from the elected representatives of the people and gives power to those who interpret the Bill of Rights, namely the currently unelected, irremovable, narrowly drawn judges. When we agree with these judges' interpretations of vague terms like 'privacy' we applaud. But the Catholic bishops would be the first to condemn the US Supreme Court's interpretation of the constitutional right of privacy in its 1973 pro-abortion decision, *Roe v. Wade*. Whether or not we incorporate a Bill of Rights into our domestic law is a complex constitutional problem. If enacted it ought to be accompanied by significant changes in court procedure and the mechanisms for appointing judges, matters on which the bishops were silent. There is no reason to believe that the bishops know what they are talking about when they recommend such half-hearted constitutional reform.

This does not stop bishops around the world from bizarre interventions in matters of law. For example, judges on California's Supreme Court have to stand for re-election by their people. An orchestrated campaign to unseat Chief Justice Rose Bird from the Court in 1987 succeeded in voting her out of office on the ground that she was 'too soft' in consistently voting against the death penalty. Where did the bishops stand on this? In disarray. The American Catholic hierarchy had taken a firm stance against the death penalty, yet Archbishop Mahoney of Los Angeles supported the campaign against the Chief Justice. These are deep jurisprudential waters, in which angels would fear to tread. If, as the Second Vatican Council said, bishops have limited expertise, their expertise must stop somewhere, perhaps at the technical merits of judges. We should not look to the hierarchy for conclusive advice on law or politics.

The law is a technique of social control. It has an important but limited role in society. It is not the be-all and end-all. It is not the preserve or speciality of the bishops. They should not be pressed for concrete solutions to every legal and political problem. The bishops ought, on the other hand, to be the experts on what *is* the be-all and end-all of life. The task for them is to establish the preconditions for the laity to apply the hierarchy's spiritual guidance to the complex temporal world. In particular, we should study the Second Vatican Council's fund of wisdom on this relationship and especially the reminder in *Gaudium et Spes* that 'Christians should recognize that various legitimate though conflicting views can be held concerning the regulation of temporal affairs.'

Again we have chosen three sample topics in which to examine the relationship of bishops to politicians. First, we look at the role of English bishops as Her Majesty's Opposition, as the only convincing, critical opposition to Thatcherism – the only constructive, alternative ideology. Then, we look at the privileges given to the bishops and their believers in their schools system; since education is nowadays so bound up with politics, this is an instructive case study on the way in which bishops attempt to manoeuvre into a powerful position in society. Finally, we look at the role of the bishops in the troubles of Northern Ireland.

Mrs Thatcher and the Bishops

The first point to make about the involvement of Anglican and Catholic bishops in British politics in opposition to Mrs Thatcher is that her Government should not feel singled out for scrutiny by the bishops. Governments all over the world are being called to account by bishops. Most notably, this is happening in Latin America where the bishops of that continent have met time and again to formulate powerful statements on the kind of justice to which they feel their flocks are entitled from politicians. The Pope has issued encyclicals which have condemned equally the Marxism he encountered as a bishop in Poland and the capitalism he now meets on his world tours.

Nor should Mrs Thatcher feel that Anglo-American bishops only started to think about politics once she and President Reagan were elected in 1979 and 1980 respectively. It is true that American bishops are wont to issue guidance at election times but only as to the most important issues of the moment and as to the general principles which should guide voters. As the American bishops stressed in their electoral advice a decade ago:

> We specifically do not seek the formation of a religious voting bloc; nor do we wish to instruct persons on how they should vote by endorsing candidates. We urge citizens to avoid choosing candidates simply on the personal basis of self-interest. Rather, we hope that voters will examine the position of candidates on the full range of issues as well as the person's integrity, philosophy and performance.

In this spirit, Bishop Kelly put the American Catholic church's view of politics to both the Democrat and the Republican platform committees in advance of the 1980 election which saw Ronald Reagan become President. The Bishop stated that there were three moral principles at the heart of Catholic teaching on social and economic justice:

> Human dignity is the criterion of a just economy and a humane world. It is protected by a set of fundamental human rights. These include the right to the basic necessities without which full human development is impossible.
>
> Pope John Paul II on his recent visit proclaimed this essential human dignity. In his address to the United Nations, for example, he said, 'Every analysis must start from the premise that ... every human being is endowed with a dignity that must never be lessened, impaired or destroyed, but it must instead be respected and safeguarded.' In enumerating basic rights

essential to human dignity, Pope John Paul listed, among others, the rights to employment, food, housing, health care and education.

The primary responsibility of the state is to serve the common good. It has a responsibility to adopt economic policies to ensure that the essential needs of all its people are met. These needs include adequate income, employment, food, shelter, health care, education and access to the necessary social services. All persons have the right to these basic necessities; and the government as the provider of last resort has the responsibility to ensure that they be made available to all.

As Christian believers, we are knowingly and willingly biased in our approach to social and economic problems. We stand with the poor and attempt to analyse public policy with a special concern for them. When their fundamental rights are in danger, we protest: when programs are offered to improve their condition, we applaud.

Hence the Anglican bishops' most published attack on Thatcherism, the *Faith in the City* report, has to be seen in its world-wide context and indeed the historical context of two thousand years of episcopal teaching on social/economical/political questions. We could, of course, go back to the Bible for early statements on these matters. But even if we confine ourselves to the last one hundred years, there has been a succession of important statements from Catholic and Anglican bishops. In the Catholic church, Pope Leo XIII's encyclical, *Rerum Novarum*, was published in 1891 and constitutes the first of the modern papal contributions to social theology. Then came Pope Pius XI's encyclical *Quadragesimo Anno* in 1931, Pope John XXIII's encyclical *Mater et Magistra* in 1961, and then Pope Paul VI's two statements – *Populorum Progressio* and his *Call to Action* on the 80th anniversary of Pope Leo's encyclical, *Octogesimi Adveniens*.

The Synod of Bishops issued its own statement, *Justice in the World*, in 1971, and regional conferences of bishops have deluged their governments and their believers with paper on these themes. The most famous of these regional episcopal statements come from Latin America, the documents from Medellin in 1968 and Puebla in 1978. But perhaps the most striking pastoral letter came from the

Catholic bishops of Appalachia in the USA, who were so distressed by the powerlessness of their people that they wrote a moving, free-verse pastoral letter entitled 'This land is home to me':

> Profit over people
> is an idol.
> And it is not a new idol,
> for Jesus long ago warned us,
>
> No one can be the slave of two masters:
> either he will hate the first
> and love the second,
> or treat the first with respect
> and the second with scorn.
> You cannot be the slave
> both of God and money.   (Matthew 6:24)
>
> This nation,
> containing about 6 per cent of the earth's population,
> consumes over one-third of the earth's energy
> and causes 40 per cent of the earth's industrial pollution . . .
>
> Some talk about a population problem
> among the poor.
> There's an even bigger consumption problem
> among the rich –
> consumption not just of luxuries,
> but of power
> of the power to shape
> – economic structures
> – political structures
> – cultural structures
> all in the service of
> – more waste
> – more profit
> – more power . . .
>
> Ironically,
> most people in this country
> are not satisfied with the consumer society.
> It makes life a rat race,
> where nobody feels they belong,

where all are pushed around,
where roots disappear,
With so much busy-ness
and clutter of thing . . .

But the children of the mountains
have fought for a different way.
Their struggles and their poetry
together keep alive

– a dream
– a tradition
– a longing
– a promise

which is not just their dream,
but the voiceless vision
buried beneath life's bitterness
wherever it is found.

They sing of a life
free and simple,
with time for one another,
and for people's needs,
based on the dignity of the human person,
at one with nature's beauty,
crowned by poetry.
If that dream dies,
all our struggles
die with it.

Of course Mrs Thatcher and President Bush might reject this poem
as economically naïve (and literary critics might urge the bishops to
keep out of poetry), but such a distinctive contribution puts in
perspective the recent challenges to the British government by the
Anglican bishops. We should *expect* bishops to speak out on behalf
of the poor, the weak, the marginalized in society. If they are to use
their voices at all, it should be as the voice of these otherwise
voiceless.

Far from being an aberration, the challenges to Thatcherism
proposed by the Anglican Bishop of Liverpool and, most famously,
the Anglican Bishop of Durham signal the way forward for our

bishops. They *ought* to be Her Majesty's Opposition, indeed *our* opposition, not because Thatcherism is necessarily wrong (John Major may well be a better Chancellor of the Exchequer than any Appalachian bishop would be), but because good government *requires* good opposition, it needs to be called to account, it needs to have its conscience pricked.

For a variety of reasons, the opposition parties in the United Kingdom over the last decade have not provided such a challenge to Thatcherism. Even if they had, they could be dismissed as partisan. The bishops, in contrast, are well placed above party politics to probe the human costs of Mrs Thatcher's regeneration of the economy, while giving due appreciation to the benefits which it has brought.

Before descending to detail, finally, we would stress a key passage in our interview with David Jenkins, the Bishop of Durham and the alleged scourge of Thatcherism. This should be borne in mind in thinking about this whole issue of the bishops' opposition to government policy. The Bishop of Durham told us that:

> It isn't good enough to say that the role of the church is to be the spokesman of the poor. The reason that the church is to be the spokesman of the poor is on the one hand to do with the fact that the poor are included in all those for whom Christ died, but also to do with the way in which, in the Old Testament, the poor are seen as a significant discerning point in a sort of prophetic utterance – the prophetic utterance was not simply about the poor, but both about society as a whole and its relation to the day of the Lord, which in modern times we would call the Kingdom of God.

The 1985 report *Faith in the City* spent half its time criticizing the church for being out of touch with life in the inner city and the other half of its time attacking government policy, calling for higher child benefit and welfare payments and more investment in job creation for the inner cities. Most controversially, the Archbishop of Canterbury's commission declared that those who were suffering in the inner cities were suffering *because* of Thatcherism – or, as the report put it, modern conservatism – in its emphasis on individualism rather than the post-war consensus of collectivism. Mrs Thatcher declared herself 'absolutely shocked' at one aspect of the

Archbishop's report, namely that it failed to make any proposals whatsoever for developing the role of individuals and families in setting standards for the society. Mrs Thatcher's supporters were more forthright, condemning virtually every aspect of the report's critique of the government, with one Cabinet Minister denouncing the whole document as 'Marxist'.

The most withering attack on *Faith in the City* came from another religious leader, the Chief Rabbi, then Sir Immanuel Jakobovits (who shortly afterwards became Lord Jakobovits). Writing in *The Times*, he took the report to task for its silence on the selfishness of trade unions and its failure to encourage blacks in the inner city to follow the example of Jews in working themselves out of their poverty. The Chief Rabbi would have preferred the document to have focused on work rather than welfare.

Not only did the Chief Rabbi receive a peerage, he then became something akin to the government's spiritual guru. For the Chief Rabbi's vision of the role of the church leader was much more in line with Mrs Thatcher's than with that of the bishops themselves. Although Mrs Thatcher's constituency, Finchley, has a significant number of Jewish voters, in the country as a whole the number of Jews led by the Chief Rabbi is small (similar to the number of members of the Church of Ireland led by Dr Eames), which shows that a sufficiently powerful religious leader can have an impact on the country's life out of all proportion to the numbers of his supporters. In contrast, the numerically strong Church of England seems to be in danger of dissipating its influence in its confrontations with the government of the day.

But again, we would argue that the prophetic quality to *Faith in the City* is beneficial to all and sundry, including Mrs Thatcher herself. For, without such critiques, Thatcherism would not have acquired its distinctive quality. Without a vigorous challenge, it would have developed no rationale other than expediency. In truth, it is the challenges of the Anglican bishops, notably the Bishop of Durham but also the Bishop of Liverpool, which have shaped Thatcherism.

Some would say that it is, on the contrary, Margaret Thatcher who has shaped the bishops' approaches to leadership. Perhaps the Prime Minister has affected our understanding of leadership in all walks of life, for better or worse. If you ask any member of the public to name a strong leader, Mrs Thatcher would be the first name and any number of bishops would come straggling a long way down the field. Yet the bishops try to impose their own style in the manner of Mrs Thatcher. They often fall into the practice of Mrs Thatcher in overshadowing their colleagues, in her case the other members of the government, in the bishops' case, their auxiliary bishops and fellow clerics. For all the pious words about facilitating the laity uttered during the National Pastoral Congress in Liverpool in 1980, Catholic bishops like Archbishop Worlock tend to dominate. The Archbishop is for ever being photographed with his Anglican twin, David Sheppard, but never with his own auxiliary bishops. He is delighted to write a book, *Better Together*, with Bishop Sheppard, but does not give his fellow Catholic bishops a higher profile by writing with them. He makes sure that his sermons and statements are distributed to the press and thus encourages attention on himself. He is not known to refer journalists to better-qualified Catholic lay people. He is the boss. This approach seems to us to owe something to Mrs Thatcher's style of management. During general election campaigns in particular, her fellow Ministers have little or no chance to answer questions at press conferences before she steps in to give her authorized version.

Not only has the Prime Minister given the bishops a few lessons on leadership, she is now concerned to give them lessons on religion. In 1988, she gave a speech cum sermon to the General Assembly of the Church of Scotland. The bishops' critics would say that this is the least they deserve for 'meddling' in politics, but it is certainly the case that the world seems to have been turned upside down with bishops preaching politics and politicians preaching religion. The thrust of Mrs Thatcher's sermon was to emphasize the notion of individual responsibility:

> We are still responsible for our own actions. We cannot blame society if we break the law. We simply cannot delegate the exercise of mercy in generosity to others. Politicians and other secular powers should strive by their measures to bring out the good in people and to fight down the bad; but they can't create the one or abolish the other.

The only unit beyond the individual which the Prime Minister seems prepared to believe in is the family. Hence she spoke of the 'basic ties of the family which are at the heart of our society and are the very nursery of civic virtue. It is on the family that we the government build our policies for welfare, education and care.' This sermon echoed an earlier interview with a women's magazine in which the Prime Minister claimed that 'there is no such thing as society, there are individual men and women and there are families'.

If this can be taken to be part of a distinctive characteristic of Thatcherism, then the bishops attack it because, as Archbishop Worlock and Bishop Sheppard have argued in *Better Together*, 'looking after number one, to use the fashionable phrase, cannot be advanced as Christian social justice'. As *Faith in the City* declared,

> the creation of wealth must go hand in hand with just distribution . . . there is a long Christian tradition reaching back into the Old Testament prophets and supported by influential schools of economic and political thought, which firmly rejects the amassing of wealth unless it is justly obtained and fairly distributed. If these provisos are not insisted upon, the creation of wealth cannot go unchallenged as a first priority of national policy.

Focusing on poverty rather than wealth, the Liverpool bishops have explained that 'the deprivation of our neighbour is a matter of concern to our *faith* [emphasis added]. There are faith-issues underlying unemployment, inadequate housing, educational disadvantage, powerlessness and hunger.' The bishops proceed to ask, 'can it seriously be contested that despair, loneliness, lack of vision and the human spirit are also faith-issues calling for the urgent attention of the Church?'

Mrs Thatcher's Scottish sermon seems to acknowledge the right of bishops to contribute to this kind of debate since she accepted that the scriptures offered 'a view of the universe, a proper attitude to work and principles to shape economic and social life'. This concession by the Prime Minister should end claims that the bishops have no right to poke their noses into politics. The debate should move to a higher plane on which we could discuss the merit, rather than the fact, of the bishops' attack on Thatcherism.

This takes us back to an earlier point, that if Thatcherism has any coherence, it has perhaps been given such shape by the need to respond to episcopal attacks on a variety of fronts. Yet there still remains the doubt as to whether Thatcherism as such exists. The last ten years have, in fact, seen a fairly random collection of – admittedly often much needed – policies which have retrospectively been blessed with the ad-men's label of Thatcherism. Yet the 1979 Conservative Party manifesto gave few clues as to the large-scale privatization, for instance, which subsequently happened and which is now considered to be at the heart of 'Thatcherism'. Rather than argue about the detail of Margaret Thatcher's economic management, the most important point to absorb about Thatcherism is its dependence on a sense of moral righteousness. It is this which the bishops challenged and that, in our opinion, is why their challenge stung the Prime Minister so deeply. Hugo Young in his mammoth account of the Thatcher years, *One of Us*, devotes little attention to the bishops (mistakenly, in our view), but he has a sure touch in identifying this key element in Thatcherism. In his words, it is

> a sense of moral rectitude ... All leaders lay claim to higher purposes, but most of them experience at least a portion of private cynicism. She was not burdened with such a feeling, at least about herself or what she was doing. The appeal to righteousness stretched much further than economic management ... The moral dimension, while a key to her dynamism, also made her blind.

Perhaps because of Mrs Thatcher's unmistakable sincerity in believing that she is in the right, other politicians have found it difficult to challenge this dynamic quality. But the bishops have no particular political axe to grind and they have been unwilling to overlook negative aspects of Thatcherism. In particular, the bishops have hammered away at their theme, that Thatcherism's supposed benefits for the poor, the theory that increased wealth will 'trickle down' to the poor, is just not true and can be shown not to have worked. This is indeed a salutary lesson for the body politic to learn.

Education

Where the interests of the present government and the bishops clash most directly is in the field of education. Margaret Thatcher's third term of office has seen schools become a battleground, and it is a conflict that the churches have entered with gusto. Whereas on questions of unemployment, inner-city deprivation and homelessness, churchmen are to an extent acting as representatives of the people – disinterested mediators – over schools they have a definite self-interest. For the churches have long realized that control of schools and a role in educating young minds is at the base of their power and authority. The idea is best summed up in the old adage attributed to the founder of the Jesuits, 'Give me a child before he's seven, and I'll show you the man'.

Some forty years ago, R. A. Butler's Education Act gave the Roman Catholic and Anglican churches and their bishops a significant role in the new national state-funded secondary school system. Now the government has initiated a far-reaching shake-up of the legacy of that landmark statute that poses a formidable challenge for today's prelates. The reaction of the two churches to this onslaught has seen a rather dramatic role reversal. The Catholic hierarchy, who fought a sustained and ultimately effective campaign in the 1930s and 1940s to win the privileged position they have enjoyed since Butler's Act, have in the late 1980s been singularly unsuccessful at defending their entrenched advantages. By contrast their Anglican counterparts, who never mustered up the strength to battle for their independence in 1944 and largely cast their lot in with the state sector, have used their status and block vote in the House of Lords to persuade – and where necessary compel – the Secretary of State for Education to show a great deal more devotion to religious education than he had envisaged in his core curriculum.

Butler's 1944 Act gave church (voluntary) schools two alternatives for their future, depending essentially on how much they were prepared to invest in secondary education. Either the state would provide full finance under 'controlled' status – where the local education authority appointed the majority of governors with church people in a minority – or the bishops could choose 'aided' status – where their appointees would hold a controlling position on the Board of Governors in exchange for their footing the bill for half of any capital expenditure (building work).

In return for their investment in 'aided' status the church would have a virtually free hand in religious education and its place on the curriculum, as well as in admissions policy. In 'controlled' establishments denominational instruction could only be given by 'reserved teachers', specifically appointed by the governors. All other staff were chosen by the local education authority.

As an educationalist remarked at the time of Butler's Act, the financial hurdle confronting the bishops if they wanted to control their schools had been placed high enough to satisfy the general public that the government was not selling out to the Catholics, and, equally, high enough to dissuade a hard-up Church of England sector from joining in what was in effect an early incarnation of 'opting out'. (Such an analysis is borne out by the fact that as soon as controversy over the concession to the Catholic church had died down sufficiently to be no longer politically damaging the 'hurdle' was reduced, with the state paying 85 per cent rather than 50 per cent of capital costs.)

'Aided' and 'controlled' schools – together with the 'voluntary' sector – account for around 30 per cent of all schools in this country. All Catholic colleges are aided, while over 65 per cent of Anglican institutions are 'controlled.'

However, it would be unfair to say that the Anglicans were simply unwilling to pay the price of the greater independence afforded by 'aided' status. The Church of England bishops in 1944, in keeping with their established position, saw their role very much as providing education for anyone in a parish who wanted it, as a service to the community regardless of belief, if any. Hence the approach of Church of England schools could not be as narrowly denominational as in Catholic alternatives if they were to conform with such a vision. A closer link with the state through 'controlled' status was more appropriate. The reinforcement of faith – preaching to the converted – was left to the Catholics in their 'aided' schools.

And it was this same lack of denominational fervour that made Church of England schools' policy an area substantially without controversy and without public intervention by the Anglican bishops for forty years. Some may have argued that Church of England establishments were no different in essence from the state secondary down the road, but the church was unmoved and no debate resulted. The bishop in charge of the Board of Education must have looked on his post as a rather comfortable sinecure, a mark of his ability to get on with children during the school visits that constituted most of the duties of his office.

Similarly, in the Catholic church there was for decades very little in the way of great educational initiatives. The Second Vatican Council of the mid-1960s brought a breath of fresh air into the classroom that blew away a somewhat stultifying concentration on personal sinfulness and in the process contributed to a better general opinion of the products of a Catholic education – even if the methods employed continue to be the stuff of folklore (what the nuns tell their convent-girls and how *Christian* brothers hit the hell out of their boys).

The appointment of Kenneth Baker as Secretary of State for Education and Science in 1986 changed that undeclared state of peace. With his core curriculum, business-funded inner-city colleges, liberalization of admissions policy and 'opting out' plans, he was in effect waving the proverbial red rag at the bishops. Some reacted with bull-like determination – most notably the Anglican Bishop of London, Dr Graham Leonard, head of the Church of England Board of Education since 1983.

Some of the reactions by the bishops to Mr Baker's radical shake-up of educational policy were decidedly negative. For instance both the Catholic dioceses of Westminster and Liverpool, the two senior centres in the country, refused to sell their redundant school buildings in the inner cities for use as City Technology Colleges – innovatory institutions, joint efforts between Whitehall and industry, designed to produce round-peg students to fit into the round-peg vacancies which business claims the current crop of squared products of comprehensives cannot fit. The Catholic bishops argued in this, as in a general critique of Mr Baker's schemes, that he was too mechanistic in his approach to education, with too little time for development of the 'whole person' whose success or failure cannot be judged in terms of examination results.

But the church did not present a united face to even this small change. The Catholic Bishop of Hexham and Newcastle, Hugh Lindsay, for example, is to allow similar inner-city church premises to be sold to a planned CTC. He prefers a wait-and-see attitude to the developments.

On the major items on Mr Baker's roll call of reforms, his most implacable opponent was without doubt Graham Leonard, Bishop of London. As the Education Reform Bill passed before the House of Lords for their scrutiny, after emerging virtually unchanged from the Commons, it found its most effective challenger not on the Labour benches but in this formidable bishop.

In his battle-strategy, the bishop had very clear objectives – and an able lieutenant in Colin Alves, his general secretary at the Board of Education. Principal amongst the targets was the all-round low marks given to RE on the core curriculum. From being the only subject guaranteed a place in the classroom in Butler's 1944 Act, it was scarcely mentioned in Baker's first draft of reforms. Bishop Leonard, who as we shall see later is a stickler for sound doctrine and rigorously argued dogma, was determined to reverse this relegation of religion's role in schools. He was in effect fighting both for the Church of England and for the Catholics in this, using his platform in the House of Lords and his personal contact with Kenneth Baker, himself a devout churchman. The complexities of a major piece of legislation meant that Bishop Leonard had to spend interminable hours in the debating chamber, as each clause was scrutinized in detail, in order to state his case with effect.

Through the Bishop's skill as a politician, the decision to exclude religion from the core curriculum was reversed by the Secretary of State, while later in the debate the Bishop of London successfully united the Christian peers spread across Labour, Democrat and Conservative benches with independents, to defy the Secretary of State and insist on a specifically Christian content in morning assemblies in schools. In this the Bishop argued that the 1944 Act had always been too vague on the point and that precision was needed. Local education authorities will retain the right to formulate syllabuses that meet the needs of children of other religious backgrounds.

As the Education Reform Bill went back to the Commons on 7 July 1988, Bishop Leonard had good reason for congratulating himself on a campaign well fought. He had taken on the government and defeated it, not on a narrow denominational point, but on what he presented as an issue of general interest to all parents with children of school-going age. Admirers and critics united in his praise – the Chief Rabbi, Lord Jakobovits, usually a staunch supporter of the government, paid tribute to the Bishop's 'enormous skill, ingenuity and persistence'.

Bishop Leonard co-operated closely with the Catholic bishops during his parliamentary campaign, and his victory was one shared in many ways with them. But, when it came to fighting their own particular corner in relation to Mr Baker's changes, the Catholic bishops apparently had neither the energy nor the broader national basis of concern and support that Dr Leonard marshalled so effectively.

Granted, they lacked his public platform in the Lords, but in their lobbying of the substantial group of Catholic peers in the House of Lords they failed even to convince such key figures as the Duke of Norfolk, usually regarded as Britain's leading Catholic layman, of the merits of their case and their fears for Catholic schools.

In successive meetings with the Secretary of State, the Catholic bishops, headed by their schools expert, Bishop David Konstant of Leeds, won only minor concessions on their control of levels of admission to Catholic schools of non-Catholics, and had no joy at all over the controversial 'opting out' proposals from which they wanted Catholic establishments to be exempted; or at least for the trustees of the Catholic schools, namely the bishops, to have a right of veto if parents and governors wanted to apply for direct funding from Whitehall. Senior Catholic churchmen talked at the time of a private undertaking by the Secretary of State not to go against their wishes in the case of a church school which wanted to opt out. If indeed such a concession ever existed, and the Department of Education for one refused to acknowledge it, it was not apparently worth the paper it was written on. Blessed Hugh More School in Mrs Thatcher's home town of Grantham in Lincolnshire was backed by its bishop trustee, James McGuinness of Nottingham, in attempts to opt out. Mr Baker turned them down.

The failure of the Catholic bishops to match their achievements of 1944 in the late 1980s when confronted with Mr Baker's plan can largely be attributed to the lack of interest his challenge prompted, initially at least, in Catholic circles. Never could the bishops threaten the Secretary of State with any substantial public disquiet, always a telling point with Ministers who have to keep an eye on the next election date. For the Catholic community, control of its own schools was apparently not the talisman or battle-cry in 1989 that it had been in the years before the Second World War. English Catholics, partly as a result of the relatively easy time they have enjoyed since 1944 in educational provision, had come out of the ghetto, and been more integrated in the general community. They were as a result less likely to fight a denominational battle over Mr Baker's changes.

It has been argued by educationalists that both the Catholic bishops and Dr Leonard have missed the point of the essential threat that Mr Baker's mechanistic and results-orientated proposals pose to church-run schools. Or at least if they are aware of it, they certainly didn't persuade their constituency, namely the parents and future parents of children at such schools, to join them in the fight.

The net result of this failure to tackle adequately the underlying drift of Mr Baker's desire to make schools in the government's own image was to give his successor as Secretary of State, John MacGregor, unprecedented powers over what goes on in church schools – largely at the expense of the bishops.

It is Mr MacGregor and his officials who control the core curriculum which Catholic and Church of England schools will be obliged to teach. The formulation of the core curriculum has been carried out within the framework of an overall notion of training for skills that will make the 'product' of schools useful in the 'free market' that awaits him or her at the age of sixteen or eighteen. The Christian ideal of development of personality, of spiritual and moral values, has necessarily been undermined. By exploiting the slogan of 'parent power', Mr Baker was able subtly to outmanoeuvre the bishops and achieve for the Secretary of State a dominant role in what goes on in schools.

But the battle is far from over yet: for the Catholic church, increasingly aware of what it lost in practical terms in the 1988 Education Reform Act, has risen from the ashes to fight again. Mr MacGregor may hold the whip hand now, but he has found a new opponent. Normally a churchman who prefers caution to polemic, and behind-the-scenes negotiations in the corridors of Whitehall to open attack on a public platform, Cardinal Basil Hume has marked the elevation of John MacGregor to the Education Ministry with a passionate demand that the new Act must be amended.

His attack on the Act is based upon its opting-out proposals which, as we saw earlier, were the bishops' major stumbling block before the plans could become law. However, the church's vacillation then has now been replaced by a dogged determination to fight, backed by support in the Catholic community.

The catalyst was a small, academically successful comprehensive in West London.The Cardinal Vaughan Memorial School in Holland Park, much favoured by the quieter sort of aristos and the arts establishment who inhabit this fashionable area of London, stood in the way of a reorganization plan for Catholic secondary education in the central and western area of Cardinal Hume's Westminster archdiocese. His proposal to remove the Vaughan's sixth form and transfer it to a tertiary college near by had the parents up in arms. Their appeals and candlelit vigils failed to move Cardinal Hume and his education advisers. So the parents decided to apply to the Secretary of State to 'opt out'.

Their overwhelming vote in favour of this course of action – an option opened up by the Education Reform Act – infuriated the Cardinal. As trustee of the school – that is the one responsible for its buildings and its Catholic ethos – he had to face the possibility of the day-to-day running being removed from his hands; or, in other words, stolen away by the parents, with the connivance of the Secretary of State.

Speaking to the National Conference of Priests in Birmingham in autumn 1989, in a speech that was to mark the start of his all-out assault on the Education Reform Act, Basil Hume outlined his dilemma over the Cardinal Vaughan School.

> When a Local Education Authority school obtains grant-maintained [opted out] status, the Local Education Authority has no further involvement with the school thereafter. But when a diocesan school (like the Cardinal Vaughan) gains grant-maintained status, the diocese remains the trustee of the school . . . despite the fact that the trustee [namely himself] may have opposed the move because it was not in the interests of the Catholic community.

Such a situation was intolerable, the Cardinal said, and he demanded a change in the law that would exempt schools under threat of reorganization from the opting-out procedure, until a decision on that reorganization had been made. Thus the opting-out clause would not be able to become an escape avenue for disgruntled parents like those at the Vaughan.

In essence, what the Cardinal was saying was what his colleagues had told Kenneth Baker eighteen months earlier, to little avail. But this time the situation was different. Not only did the Cardinal

Vaughan School present a clear example of the absurdity of the legislation from the point of view of the Catholic authorities, but the battle in West London had animated Catholics all around the country in defence of their Cardinal and, by association, of their schools.

Principal in this awakening to the dangers posed by the Conservative government's education reforms was the spectacle of the Cardinal himself stating publicly his willingness to go to prison for his beliefs. When the Cardinal Vaughan School application to opt out had been drawn up by the parents, it needed the Cardinal as trustee to name the governors of the school, before the relevant papers could be forwarded to the Secretary of State. This Basil Hume refused to do, with a de-Gaulle-like finality. He would rather end up in court and possibly in prison for refusing to carry out what the Education Reform Act made a legal duty, he told the Catholic community.

His stance had the desired effect of bringing the whole question of the position of the church in opting-out battles to public attention. Newspaper headlines talked of a clash between church and state. The Catholic community was alerted and rallied to such an extent that when, several weeks later, he backed down on his threat to go to court, his campaign lost none of its impetus.

In his speech to the National Conference of Priests, referred to earlier, he stepped up the pressure on Catholics in Britain to support him by accusing them of apathy over the future of the same Catholic schools that only forty years ago had been the sole focus of attention and fund-raising in many parishes.

His determination couldn't fail to make an impact on John MacGregor, the new Secretary of State. Although talk of a church–state clash was exaggerated, the power and the passion which the subject of Catholic schools can generate was once again demonstrated at just the time it appeared to be on the wane. Just as Graham Leonard was able to make Kenneth Baker compromise, Basil Hume seems on course to exact concessions from John MacGregor.

The battle for control of the schools is even more marked in Northern Ireland, where the Catholic bishops are often seen as the major obstacle to integrated education. When a new Apostolic Nuncio arrived in Dublin in 1989, he was asked at the airport whether he approved of integrated schools for Northern Ireland.

He gave such schools his whole-hearted approval, as any outsider would do, and was then flabbergasted to be told it was his Catholic bishops who were opposing such developments.

There seems to be an irony here. Catholic bishops have been at the forefront of demands for fair (integrated) employment. Yet there is a limit to what the law can achieve in promoting an integrated workforce in a society which has segregated housing, schooling and socializing. Part of this segregation is caused by different religious denominations choosing to base their social lives, and their children's schooling, around their churches. Part of the segregation is caused by past or present differences in economic well-being. Part of the segregation, particularly in relation to housing, is explicable by intimidation or fear. If segregation is the problem, then why not follow the American example of the US Supreme Court decision in 1954, *Brown* v. *Board of Education*, and the subsequent bussing controversy, by desegregating the schools? *Brown* was the famous case which ended the doctrine of 'separate but equal' and insisted that if the USA was to live up to its Fourteenth Amendment which requires equal protection of the laws for all citizens, regardless of colour or race, then schools had to be integrated. So, why not export this proposal to Northern Ireland? Integrate the schools and Protestants and Catholics will live together happily ever after.

The answer is that the two contexts are very different. In the USA up to the 1950s (and sometimes beyond) blacks were not *allowed* to go to white schools. In Northern Ireland, however, the minority Catholics are allowed to go to any school they wish. But they *choose* to attend their own denominational schools. Their bishops seem to insist that they segregate themselves. They are, moreover, entitled to do so according to European notions of human rights. Article 2 of the First Protocol to the European Convention on Human Rights guarantees the right to choose religious education: 'No person shall be denied the right to education. In the exercise of any functions which it assumes in relation to education and to teaching, the state shall respect the right of parents to ensure such education and teaching in conformity with their own religious and philosophical convictions.' Hence the UK government could not impose integrated schooling in Northern Ireland without violating the rights of the Catholic minority whom the measure would supposedly be protecting.

So the issue is far more complex than in the USA. In particular, Catholics pride themselves on their schooling; in a society which discriminated against them for fifty years, the schools were one haven in which Catholics controlled their own destiny. For that reason alone, one can see that today's Catholic bishops in Northern Ireland are reluctant to give up that heritage and abandon their own schools, even if liberal reformers feel that it would be in their people's own long-term interests to attend integrated schools. Of course, there are other less worthy reasons for maintaining the separate school system, such as the enormous financial and institutional commitment to Catholic education. And there is no doubt in many minds that segregated schooling contributes to lack of understanding between different religious groups. A sense of division and fear of the unknown arises simply from the fact of different groups being educated in different schools.

The government is clearly prepared to incur the wrath of the Catholic bishops and is beginning to support movements for integrated education. Precisely because of the *de facto* segregation of communities and the strength of feeling about denominational schools, however, integrated education is only a plausible goal in certain parts of Northern Ireland. There will always be areas where the other side are so far away that only marathon bussing could provide 'balanced' schools. But the government is entitled to think seriously about the extent to which it offers incentives for the creation of new integrated schools. At present, the government is encouraging such schools, much to the annoyance of Catholic bishops and Catholic and state schools who feel that they are being pushed to the back of the queue for educational funds.

The argument for giving integrated schools priority is rather like the argument, which Catholic bishops would accept, for affirmative action in the sphere of employment. In the past, those who would have chosen integrated education did not have the option, so there is a lot of time, money and effort to be made up in favour of those who are prepared to cross divides. Integrated schools suffer three handicaps in Northern Ireland: the first is precisely that they are seen as challenging religious isolation; the second is that they are, by definition, new in a society which has many schools of long-standing academic excellence; third, perhaps because of the 'liberal' views of those who are likely to send their children to them, they are associated in Northern Ireland with comprehensive schooling rather than the selective, grammar-school education which still prevails in Northern Ireland despite its virtual evaporation in England. For these reasons integrated schools are unlikely to sweep across Northern Ireland to the exclusion of segregated schools. So the focus of government action in this area should be not only on integrated schools but also on integrity-in-education, even when schooling is carried out on a segregated basis. Here the bishops have been more supportive.

In June 1989, the Northern Ireland Office did indeed issue reports on such 'integrity' in education. They have developed programmes, called Education for Mutual Understanding (EMU) and Cultural Heritage, which should make a positive contribution. Moreover, the draft education order issued at the same time suggests that the government is continuing in its efforts to support the development of integrated education. As we have indicated, the former development is perhaps even more important than the latter in that it will reach *all* children in Northern Ireland. Indeed, this reform will be able to reach and touch the future generations of Northern Ireland in a way that their bishops ought to applaud. For the lessons of EMU and Cultural Heritage are the lessons which all the bishops have been preaching: respect for other traditions while celebrating one's own. It looks as if the government is taking a welcome initiative to match the bishops' words with educational actions.

The Catholic bishops need to come to terms with integrated schools. Presently, their attitude is reported as at best feigned indifference, at worst outright hostility and obstructionism (e.g. in relation to administering the sacraments to pupils who are undoubtedly adequately prepared but whose only 'crime' is that their parents have chosen a non-Catholic school for them). Such obstructionism seems paltry. Much better service to all the people of Northern Ireland and much better public relations for the church itself would be provided by the bishops emphasizing that, while their schools offer something distinctive, those who in good conscience choose to build bridges to other religious communities will also be supported by the bishops.

The Irish bishops, however, seem to disagree. Perhaps their views can best be understood in the context of an assessment of their overall contribution to the politics of Northern Ireland.

Irish Bishops

The New Ireland Forum of 1983 and 1984 included the remarkable sight, carried on television, of a delegation of the Irish Episcopal Conference being cross-examined by politicians. Bishop Cahal Daly had begun with what many politicians clearly regarded as the amazingly unrealistic statement that:

> The Catholic church in Ireland totally rejects the concept of a confessional state. We have not sought and we do not seek a Catholic state for a Catholic people. We believe that the alliance of church and state is harmful for the church and harmful for the state. We rejoiced when the ambiguous formula regarding the special position of the Catholic church was struck out of the Constitution by the electorate of the Republic.

Deputy Kelly wondered whether the bishops would oppose the removal of the constitutional ban on divorce if miraculously there should one day be a United Ireland. Bishop Daly said that this was 'a political question which is not appropriate for us to answer'. Deputy Kelly replied, 'It is not a political question, but I do agree that it is probably the first time since St Patrick arrived that the representatives of the hierarchy were asked to think on their feet.'

Catholic bishops have received a bad press in London when they have commented or failed to comment upon events in Northern Ireland. The bishops on both sides of Northern Ireland's troubles, particularly the Catholic bishops, are often criticized for failing to control their believers. But this criticism seems unfair. It is dubious, to say the least, to describe terrorists as believers in the first place. It is naïve to believe that the bishops can control the men of violence. It is thought, however, that the bishops can undermine any support there might be for the men of violence among true believers. So why don't the Catholic bishops of Ireland excommunicate members of the IRA? Why don't they condemn terrorism?

Well, of course, they have in the past excommunicated members of the IRA and perhaps they should do so again. But there is some theological sense in their reluctance to use this weapon of excommunication. The idea behind excommunicating somebody, for example arch-traditionalist Archbishop Lefebvre, is to make someone who is a believer, but who is in error, sit up and take notice of what the church is saying so that they can be welcomed back into the fold. Excommunication is not meant as a symbol to the outside world of the church's disapproval of those people who are completely unmoved by the church's stance.

That is the bishops' explanation for their current refusal to invoke excommunication as part of their struggle against terrorism. It may be, however, that this is too much of a purist's position. Given that excommunication is seen differently by the outside world, perhaps the bishops should reconsider their attitude.

Another point that the Catholic bishops of Ireland would make in this regard is that the very people who call for them to excommunicate so-called Catholic terrorists will in the next breath be condemning the Catholic bishops for their control of their people. Catholics in Northern Ireland and even more so in the Republic of Ireland are often criticized for being dominated by their bishops. Yet, when the bishops refuse to act in a heavy-handed way, they too are criticized.

So why don't the bishops at least condemn the violence? The answer is that, of course, they *do* constantly condemn the violence. The English media very seldom carry these messages. For instance, on Monday, 13 March 1989 Bishop Cahal Daly preached at the Requiem Mass for Jim McCartney, who had been shot dead by the Protestant Action Force on the previous Friday. The next day's *Irish News*, published in Northern Ireland, carried the sermon in great detail, but not one of the English papers mentioned it. It is worthwhile, therefore, setting the record straight by quoting the Bishop of Down and Connor from the sermon above, who spoke directly to the leaders of the IRA and those who could influence them, saying:

> Enough is enough. You have suffered yourselves, but the Catholic community who you like to call your own people have suffered much more than you because of your activities. They have suffered too much. Those that you call your own people are longing for the day when you call off your armed campaign. I beg you to call off your campaign, set your neighbours free from the scourge of your violence, give your people peace. Even the Ayatollah Khomeini called off the war with

Iraq when he saw that his own people were bleeding and suffering and doomed to go on suffering and bleeding more than their opponents. A character in a Sean O'Casey play remarks that it is no longer a question of the IRA dying for the Irish people, but of Irish people dying for the IRA.

Cynics will say that, while Bishop Daly may be as blunt as that at funerals, the Irish bishops on other occasions, and their leader Cardinal O'Fiaich in particular, speak with forked tongues. By encouraging demands for a United Ireland, they are legitimizing (however unintentionally) all who seek a United Ireland, even those who seek it by force. Thus, Cardinal O'Fiaich was denounced in terms ranging from 'the unacceptable face of Irish nationalism' to 'the ecclesiastical wing of the IRA' when he called, in November 1989, on the British government to say to Northern Ireland's Protestants, 'look, we are not going to stay here for all time'. The Cardinal's position seemed to challenge the Anglo-Irish Agreement, which is based on the principle that the majority of people in Northern Ireland should determine their own future.

Yet, Cardinal O'Fiaich has clearly denounced terrorism on literally hundreds of occasions. For example, in the wake of the IRA's murder of two top RUC policemen on 20 March 1989, Cardinal O'Fiaich said: 'No Catholic can join or remain a member of any organization which perpetrates such evil deeds.'

We have made clear, however, that the basis of Christian belief is tied up with *acting* in a Christ-like manner, that actions speak louder than words. In this political sphere we are drawn back to the wise words of Pope Paul VI in his encyclical *Populorum Progressio*, 'Peace cannot be limited to a mere absence of war ... peace is something that is built up day after day, in the pursuit of an order intended by God, which implies a more perfect form of justice among men.' So we can legitimately ask: what have the Anglican and Catholic bishops in Ireland *done* to pave the way for peace? Indeed, we did ask Anglican and Catholic bishops in Ireland exactly that question. In order to examine their role as peacemakers and to look at the ways in which other bishops seek to fulfil their mission, we will now sketch some impressions of selected bishops in action.

Part III

Visions

———

The first bishops of the Christian church were the twelve apostles. None of them would be likely to be made a bishop today. They didn't go to the right universities. They would not have been impressive on television. They were ordinary men. Yet Christ chose them to be leaders, teachers and shepherds to his flock. He entrusted his church to their care and to that of their successors down through the ages to our current bishops. Although society has changed dramatically, today's bishops are still subject to that same threefold imperative that inspired them: to care for, to guide and ultimately to lead the church. Although each of today's bishops has a different interpretation of his office, of the scriptural and theological bases that underpin and sustain it, these are all variations on that central mission entrusted to the apostles.

In examining the work of individual bishops, we have grouped them under the headings of prophets, and pastors and peacemakers. No category is exclusive, no bishop falls wholly into one or the other. But we believe that the public debate about the future leaders of the English churches will be enriched by reflection on the terms 'prophets' and 'pastors'. The problems they have are different.

First, the laity, the media and the bishops themselves seem to have great difficulty in accepting the role of prophet. We don't like to be challenged by prophets. That is why they are without honour in their own country.

Second, while we all do accept the role of the clergy as pastors, we do not understand exactly what it entails. Shepherds used not to have Filofaxes full of committee meetings and world-wide appointments. How can today's bishops fulfil their pastoral role, particularly those who head not only a diocese but a national church?

We conclude this part by questioning whether a way forward can be found by looking outside the British experience. Are there bishops elsewhere who have successfully integrated the roles of prophet and pastor?

7

Prophets

———

Prophets can trace their role back to the Old Testament tradition of a 'voice crying in the wilderness', such as as Isaiah, Jeremiah and Daniel. This gift of prophecy was transformed by Jesus in his guidance to his apostles into a leadership role within the Christian community and within society at large.

This change between Old and New Testament notions of prophecy finds eloquent expression in both the person and the writings of St Peter, the first leader of the church. In his second letter, Peter instructs his readers that 'You will be right to depend on prophecy and take it as a lamp for lighting a way through the dark until the dawn comes and the morning star rises in your mind.'

Durham

Since his appointment in 1984 as Bishop of Durham, the fourth most senior figure in the hierarchy of the Church of England, David Jenkins has clearly taken up the challenge of St Peter to be a lamp lighting the way. As he told us:

> Well, it may sound a bit portentous, but I understand my role as a bishop as being in some sense a responsible follower and up to a point successor of the apostles, which I interpreted on my election as meaning you have a responsibility for leading the people of God in your charge on the pilgrimage of faith. And I have always associated being an apostolic follower with being some sort of pioneer and explorer.

As a senior figure in the established church, David Jenkins feels that he must give voice to that pioneering drive not only in the affairs of his diocese and communion, but on a national scale as well. His vision of the church is not one that accepts any sense of it being removed or apart from the society in which it operates. When such a determination to engage the world is combined with an ability to perform on radio and television, we arrive at the essence of the controversy that has dogged David Dunelm (as he signs himself) from the day, just weeks after his election, when part of York Minster was destroyed by fire. His critics alleged at the time that this was an act of God's displeasure at the Bishop's progressive stance.

David Jenkins has, of necessity, grown sanguine about the barrage of abuse to which he is periodically subjected. He recognizes that it is often his own actions, his own vision of the bishop as a prophet, that draws such criticism:

> People in the Church of England do not expect a follower of the apostles to go pioneering off into the distance and pursuing and all that. The notion of pioneer to them is not the prophet, but something like protector and fairly conservative pastor.

Fairly conservative – whether with a small c or a capital C, whether in politics or theology – is not a label that sits happily with the Bishop of Durham. As discussed in an earlier chapter, David Jenkins has been the Thatcher government's most hostile critic, savaging their policies on a range of issues, from the handling of the miners' strike, the economy, bus deregulation, through to more general trends like the creation of a 'yuppie' society. David Jenkins, however, refuses all attempts to pigeonhole his views or give them a party-political tag. He takes his authority from the gospels, not from any political creed, and interprets them in the light of the experiences of the people in his essentially working-class diocese.

The Tory benches in the House of Commons have ignored such subtleties and have dismissed David Jenkins's view as 'Militant Tendency at prayer'. They have dubbed the Bishop himself as 'the anti-Christ', a 'dotty clergyman' and a 'Marxist'. He refuses to meet their personal attacks in kind. While he has described Mrs Thatcher's policies as 'wicked' (in a much discussed Easter 1988 sermon), he has avoided any public condemnation of the Prime Minister herself.

David Jenkins deals with most of the abuse that rains down on his head with an air of resignation and a rather saintly smile. It is the price of speaking out for Christian values, for being a pioneer or explorer in an age that does not welcome those who step out of line, those who challenge the prevailing wisdom. His treatment in many ways mirrors the rejection of the Old Testament prophets by their people. In the New Testament, of course, Christ himself noted on the basis of personal experience that a prophet is without honour in his own country.

Yet some of the gibes that have greeted the Bishop's public statements must have hurt. Lord Hailsham's description of him as 'intellectually limited' in an address to the Carlton Club was characteristically forthright, arrogant and wrong. Before his election to the Cathedral of St Cuthbert in 1984 David Jenkins had cut a dash on the academic circuit that few other churchmen could match. With a string of influential publications to his name, he was, from 1979 until his elevation to Durham, Professor of Theology at Leeds University. Indeed many of his most controversial interventions on matters of faith – questioning the reality of the Virgin Birth or the Resurrection, for example – have shown him trying to use the language of the academic world in a wider context. This, coupled with his tendency once in front of a TV camera to think aloud, and hence back himself into corners when faced with the less than subtle approach of interviewers, has undoubtedly played its part in his fame or notoriety.

But an essential part of David Jenkins's pioneering approach to being a bishop results from that previous life in academae where he was paid to think (incidentally, there is a tradition that the see of Durham is often headed by a theologian). But he would also claim that his inquiring mind goes back a lot further than his professional life, to his Evangelical childhood:

> It has been natural from the earliest things I remember to approach anything I was interested in with an inquiring mind. I've always found asking questions a positive and hopeful thing to do. I don't claim any credit for it. It just happened that way – like the elephant child with an insatiable curiosity in the *Just So* stories of Rudyard Kipling . . . although of course the elephant child got into trouble and got engaged with a crocodile.

This is rather an apt image for many of David Jenkins's most public clashes. Whether he is debating a point at issue in the Church of

England's theology, or addressing a pressing political matter, the Bishop of Durham is constantly being dragged into the jaws of the crocodile of the largely hostile media. It is a measure of his determination to force an often reluctant church to engage in a dialogue with the world that he does not shy away from journalists. Perhaps his daughter, a BBC producer, has encouraged him in his abiding belief in the power of newspapers and television in getting a message across:

> I feel that an isolated church, an isolated theology and an isolated liturgy soon switches off the liveliness of God. My understanding of discipleship, of following Christ, is very much as being on a way to The Way. Therefore exploration, experimentation simply seem to me to be a part of what it is to be a Christian.

This explains why critics see David Jenkins as looking for controversy, whereas he sees himself as simply pursuing his vision of what it is to be a bishop, to be going forward, even if that brings dispute in its wake.

In judging David Jenkins the pioneer it is important to remember that he has carried his flock with him. He has been attacked by his fellow bishops and was even once urged to resign by Maurice Wood, a retired Bishop of Norwich. Senior Anglican politicians have dubbed him a 'musical-hall turn'. Yet his popularity in his diocese of Durham is immense.

Part of this has to do with his office and the duties it entails – parish visits, or 'mingling in the bun fight' as he puts it, keep him in touch. So does his network of communications that links him to his rural deans and then his vicars, a set-up he prefers to see as a circle with himself sitting at the centre, rather than leading from above.

Much more important is the fact that the people of Durham recognize David Jenkins's Christianity. They may not agree wholeheartedly with his views, but he has earned their respect by his attention to their needs and to the issues that affect them. Hence they, unlike his critics, can see that his appearance on a Labour party platform should not be taken so much as an endorsement of that political organization, but rather as a mark of his concern at the damage which he thinks government legislation has been doing to his flock.

The demonstrations and the protests that marred his arrival at the bishop's palatial residence, Auckland Castle, soon subsided. Talk of his being banned from certain churches in the diocese died out. 'I don't think there's a church in the diocese that's a no-go area now,' says Archdeacon Michael Perry. 'He's won them round.'

The Bishop himself makes light of the initial hostility he encountered:

> The problem soon went away with all but a very few people once they had heard what I had to say from the pulpit. Of course you have to bear in mind that very many of my congregation would have the greatest sympathy with my alleged political views. So ordinary people were prepared to give me the benefit of the doubt, partly because they suspected that I was raising the right questions, and partly because they'd rather have a bishop who is heard than one who isn't. And then there's the fact that I'm lively and as a fellow bishop said right at the beginning, 'People are not always sure of what you're saying, but they're sure you're enthusiastic and churchmanlike.'

And there is, within the national set-up of the Church of England, widespread support for much of what David Jenkins has to say. It is simply his manner and place of saying it that worries the majority of his fellow bishops. We would give him the credit for the questioning of the nature of belief and of being a bishop that led to the 1987 report from the Anglican hierarchy. Far from being, as the tabloids would have it, the man who is hell-bent on destroying faith, he has in fact led to the church's giving renewed and clear guidelines as to what it means to be an Anglican in the 1980s and beyond.

Liverpool

The Bishop of Durham has done this on his own initiative. He has led from the front. It was the Bishop of Durham who took his prophetic Christian message to the people of his diocese. They were initially hostile. But it was the Bishop who convinced them of his own sincerity and the value of his sometimes controversial pioneering message. By contrast it has been the people of Liverpool who have sought out their bishops, brought them out of their cathedrals, and nominated them as spokesmen for their troubled city. The two prelates, by the will of the people, are playing a central part in the economic, social and political life of Merseyside that has no parallel in England (although perhaps it has in Northern Ireland).

In the early Christian church the community elected its own leaders: they emerged by popular acclaim. One sees echoes of this in Liverpool. Although Anglican Bishop David Sheppard and Catholic Archbishop Derek Worlock were not placed in their sees by the community that now treasures them, they have in effect emerged by the will of the people of the city as their leaders, their spokesmen, taking on the mantle of prophets, pointing a way forward in the political and social vacuum that has gripped the area in recent times.

In their joint autobiography, *Better Together*, the two bishops define their role in regard to the city as following the people's lead: 'The true prophet must himself try to follow the way of the servant.'

Such a function as servant of the community produces in Derek Worlock's mind a model for action as a bishop that is modern, geared to contemporary needs, but which equally harks back to the earliest traditions of leadership in the Christian church:

> As a bishop you have to ensure that people have the dignity of making responsible decisions. That doesn't mean to say that you have to be indecisive or woolly. But it does mean that you've got to give the people the opportunity to see their way forward in the light of the gospel. That light of the gospel and the shedding of it might mean that I have to walk out in front. But it doesn't always mean that. It can mean walking beside the fellow with your hand on his shoulder, to encourage him to find his way to Christ.

This is a telling image for the approach of David Sheppard and Derek Worlock to being a bishop in a troubled city like Liverpool. They have stood four-square alongside the community with their hands on its shoulder, encouraging it forward. As unemployment figures have risen as high as 60 to 80 per cent in some areas of this once thriving port, as factories have followed one another into disuse, as the local council has engaged in a doomed political struggle with Whitehall over rates and services, the bishops have formed an alliance with the people that has steered the city away from disaster. The two bishops have been the spokesmen, acting with the authority of the population of Liverpool in an attempt to rebuild both the fabric and the self-confidence of Merseyside. A graphic illustration of this role came at the time of the Toxteth riots in 1981 and their aftermath when it was the bishops who were out on the streets at the height of the crisis, and it was the bishops who argued with Michael Heseltine and other government figures for assistance in ensuring that such an eruption of discontent did not happen again.

Derek Worlock and David Sheppard arrived within a year of each other in the mid-1970s to head the Catholic and Anglican dioceses of Liverpool. They came from very different backgrounds. David Sheppard is the handsome England cricketing hero, with an easy, affable manner in both public and private, who had achieved a widely acclaimed triumph first as a priest and then as a bishop in the deprived inner-city areas of east and south London. Derek Worlock is by contrast the habitual number-two batsman. Initially turned down by his bishop for the priesthood because his parents were neither Irish nor cradle Catholics, he was eventually accepted by Westminster diocese and went on to spend almost twenty years as secretary to three cardinal archbishops there. He then spent just over a year in a parish before his elevation to the bishopric of Portsmouth (the one that had rejected him all those years before), and in the months prior to his arrival in Liverpool was passed over for the leadership of the Catholic church in England despite being the most obvious candidate.

The two bishops' arrival in Liverpool coincided with a crisis in the fortunes of the city and its people. Economic and social disintegration daily brought to the doors of the two bishops' houses many requests and pleas for action. They very quickly decided on a common approach: 'It just became increasingly clear that in attempting to show the light of Christ's gospel on the problems facing Merseyside we should try wherever possible to speak with one voice,' they write in their autobiography of those first days in the city.

Whatever the historic differences and divisions between their churches at a national and international level, and in the context of a city like Liverpool that earlier this century was every bit as sectarian as present-day Belfast, the two bishops put local needs and the imperative to act effectively first. As David Sheppard explains:

I think that flows naturally out of the kind of God I believe in. I don't believe in a God who is simply for when you fold your hands in prayer. He is a creator God who cares about the quality of life that all human beings experience. I also take very seriously the whole line of the Old Testament prophets. When you want to know what the Lord means when he talks about the Kingdom of God in the gospels, then I think you have to go back to the prophets both to discover their concern for the knowledge of God, and for justice. And in the course of our concern for a whole community we see a lot of things that are very damaging to human beings, and especially if it is groups of people with very little clout, to whom nobody will listen, then it is right for us to provide a voice so that those concerns are heard.

The role played by the two bishops in voicing the concerns of Merseyside has been likened to that of joint Lord Mayors of the city. But that description, although it conveys the apolitical nature of their leadership, misses the point of their prophecy, their vision of how the ministry works in the community, by the will of the community. Scarcely a week passes when they are not involved in some round of talks about future industrial or caring schemes in the city. They host a forum, the Michaelmas group, of local businessmen, and they welcome government Ministers who come to talk about what needs to be done in concrete terms on Merseyside. That most unbending of former Cabinet Ministers, Norman Tebbit, is said to have been so moved by the bishops' 1985 statement on the 'indignity of unemployment' that he fought for extra funds for job creation in Liverpool.

For Derek Worlock this role in the community is based on the central idea that came from the Second Vatican Council's keynote document *Lumen gentium* ('The Light of the People') of an equality amongst Christ's people whether cardinals, bishops or men and women in the pews.

The key word in it all is relationship. Relationships in the church have developed in a new profundity, and the separation that was almost segregation between the different orders of the church has to a great extent disappeared. You can't say now that there is total social equality, equality of brilliance, or equality of opportunity, but there is an equality of dignity with the different ministries of the church of mutual service to one another.

David Sheppard too finds inspiration for his work in Liverpool in the recent theology of his church. Reflecting on the 1987 statement by the bishops of the Church of England, *The Nature of Christian Belief*, he highlights a particular phrase: 'It says that the bishop is both the guardian of the faith and the guardian of the exploration. And there are times when you actually have to go out and be explorers.' And the exploration undertaken by the two bishops of their office has had national consequences. The most obvious has been in presenting a positive image of their adopted city. But then there has been their effect on how both their churches, and Christians together, are seen in society. For David Sheppard his achievement in Merseyside has given the lie to talk in Anglican circles that their church was dying out in the urban areas:

> We have in the past been too much a middle-class church. My predecessor as Bishop of Woolwich said to me in 1969 when he handed over that he didn't believe there would be an inner-city church in ten years' time. I remember thinking well I'm going to do my damnedest to prove you wrong.

In Catholic circles Derek Worlock too has been a pioneer. Faced with a crisis in Liverpool, he has been unwilling to concentrate on the generalized non-specific references to the next world that have traditionally set Catholic leaders apart from their people. He has chosen, sometimes quite literally, to get his hands dirty. He has taken bold initiatives, not least in his partnership with Bishop Sheppard (whose title to episcopal office is regarded by the Vatican as null and void according to papal teaching of the last century). Derek Worlock has moved beyond such minutiae to give Catholic commitment to ecumenical progress practical expression. Some say that his pioneering in Liverpool has cost him the chance of further advancement in the Catholic church. Before he had made his mark in Liverpool, it was suggested that he might eventually take over from Cardinal Hume, or at least be awarded a cardinal's hat by Rome. But prophets are unlikely to endear themselves to promotion boards.

In the Anglican church, David Jenkins on the left, David Sheppard in the middle and Graham Leonard on the right are all talented prophets. David Sheppard may be offered the opportunity to become the next Archbishop of York (although he may equally well decline it in order to stay in Liverpool). But the other two prophets have no chance of becoming the Archbishop of Canterbury.

We have stressed that any good bishop will be not only a prophet but also a pastor and a peacemaker. We have separated the three aspects merely to highlight their distinctive elements. We also invite readers to reflect on their experience of bishops, and of these bishops in particular, to challenge our categorization. In particular, we imagine that Sheppard and Worlock might regard themselves as pastors or peacemakers rather than prophets. Their favourite word to describe their own missions seems to be 'reconciliation', the role of the peacemaker. So why have we classified them as prophets?

The answer is important to our general thesis about the role of bishops as distinct from party politicians, social workers and others with positions of responsibility in society. Lots of people seek peace and justice. Lots of people care for others. But what distinguishes bishops from secular society, or ought to, is the *spiritual* dimension to their conciliatory endeavours. Enter the role of the prophet, who is motivated by a belief in God and who seeks to convert his followers to a heavenly path. One does not have to be a religious mystic to understand the different motivation behind Derek Worlock and Derek Hatton, for example, in their roles as representatives of Liverpool.

This is not to deny an element of vanity in the two bishops' relationship with the media (although when God was handing out vanity Derek Hatton was clearly ahead of them in the queue). Some critics have told us that the bishops encourage media tags or nicknames, e.g. 'Fish and Chips' (always together and never out of the newspapers).

But there has to be an element of prayer, or spirituality, in a bishop's response to the issues of our time. In their joint autobiography the Liverpudlian bishops explain the way in which they bring a spiritual dimension into their social concerns *and* use their pastoral insights to deepen their spirituality by quoting the late Father John Dalrymple, who wrote:

> The journey inwards is the journey from the issues of this world towards God. It is a journey towards the mind of Christ, beyond feelings of expediency or fear of what people will say, to truth itself. It is followed by the journey outwards, back from the depths where we meet God, to the issues facing us in our everyday life, a journey which we now undertake with a new sensitivity to the will of God in all things.

The two bishops call this a 'two-way journey'. Significantly for our classification, their gloss on Father Dalrymple's message runs as follows:

> The two-way journey is to be recognized in the twin theme of the Old Testament prophets, who spoke of the knowledge of God and of his concern that justice should reign in his whole kingdom. Both inward and outward journeys may be pressing, but they are not always equally attractive, nor easily understood. Part of the mission of the church is, by the evidence of its priorities, to be a reminder of different values.

What is, we hope, prophetic about the two bishops' contribution to this two-way journey is that they undertake their pilgrimage inwards and outwards precisely as a twosome. Again we have already emphasized the importance of judging bishops by their actions, not just by their words, and these two bishops exemplify the rationale of that criterion. For every time they intervene as pastors or peacemakers, by the very act of intervening together, they are making a prophetic statement about the future unity of Christ's church.

London

At the end of the beatitudes, his clarion call to Christian living, Jesus speaks of how 'they persecuted the prophets before you' for speaking out in defence of what they considered to be the truth. If the Bishop of Durham has been persecuted by the media and politicians for his outspoken prophetic vision of a Christian society, Graham Leonard, the Bishop of London and the third most senior prelate in the Church of England behind Canterbury and York, has suffered a similar fate at the hands of his fellow clerics and his flock. Like David Jenkins, the Bishop of London has repeatedly stood up for his views and spoken out when his more cautious colleagues would have preferred him to remain silent. Both bishops have at times seemed close to that Old Testament image of the prophet as a voice crying in the wilderness.

But when David Jenkins has taken a stand it has been on the whole thrust of Christian belief and its application to, in his view, a largely un-Christian Thatcherite society. Graham Leonard by contrast has fought his corner on the no less headline-grabbing question of women priests. But this matter is largely an internal one; his adversaries have been his fellow bishops, not government Ministers, and the result has been less the closing of ranks seen around David Jenkins in the face of media attacks than the growing isolation of Graham Leonard from his colleagues. The gulf that divides him from the vast majority of the rest of the House of Bishops is one that he acknowledges: 'But I feel I am supported by the witness and prayers of the saints who have experienced such isolation to a far greater degree.'

So far in the chapter our image of a prophet has been that of a pioneer, of someone urging church and community forward. Graham Leonard's view of his role as a prophet is somewhat more conservative, concerned with rediscovering eternal truths:

I believe that true radicalism comes from the application of orthodox doctrines to the contemporary situation, both in the church and in the world. It follows that I see one of my major responsibilities as the teaching of the interpretation of such doctrine, drawing out its implications. In this sense, I see the role of a bishop as prophet and explorer. I am not sure I would use the description 'pioneer' with the notion of discovering what is new. But it may be justified in these days when liberalism regards pioneering as bringing back ancient heresies in modern form. There is a need for pioneering in the sense of taking the initiative to rediscover the eternal truth of the gospel.

The principal 'heresy' of those liberals of course is their willing-ness to ordain women as priests. As we have seen in an earlier chapter, Graham Leonard's weapon in combating that 'heresy' has been his constant and literal reference to Christ's teaching and example. Time after time in the twice-yearly debates of the General Synod, with a remorseless logic that a colleague has described as reminiscent of Enoch Powell in his heyday, Graham Leonard has argued that the Anglican communion is giving in to the wishes of women at the cost of ignoring the teachings of the scriptures, and substituting in their place the contemporary and therefore the tran-sitory as criteria for action.

As the debate has progressed on an international and domestic stage, however, the Bishop of London's voice has increasingly been that of the Old Testament prophet crying in the wilderness. It has been an outspokenness wholly unwelcome to the vast majority of his fellow bishops. Where they prefer progress and meeting the world on its terms, Dr Leonard strikes a chord amongst a section of the laity and clergy at least by sticking to an unshakeable belief in his own wisdom on this most crucial of subjects. He deeply resents being cast as the conservative, the die-hard obstacle to reform, arguing cogently that it is rather the modernists who should be convincing their audience of the case in favour of women on the basis of scripture. He has cast himself in the role of prophet for the *status quo*, and has somewhat reluctantly now found himself the leader on a world-wide scale of the anti-female-ordination lobby in the Anglican communion.

In view of Graham Leonard's habit of reminding the Church of England of arguments it would rather forget, what is surprising is that he has risen so far in its hierarchy. One might even take it as the positive side of the church's most publicized habit of tolerating differing opinions within its ranks. After an early Evangelical upbringing, Graham Leonard has firmly aligned himself with the high wing. His biographer, John Peart-Binns, is not alone in remarking on the Bishop's liking for popish regalia: 'He enjoys wearing purple, sometimes looking like an out-of-date Roman Catholic bishop.' Yet it is also important to note that in his diocesan posts Dr Leonard has always enjoyed a healthy working relation-ship with the Evangelicals in his flock.

As a bishop, the driving force behind Graham Leonard's rise

through the ranks has been his ability to argue his corner with a ruthless intellectual rigour. When he addresses Synod, it is as if a doubt has never crossed his mind as to the rightness of what he is saying, and in that confidence he has the capacity to turn a debate. As Suffragan Bishop of Willesden he was one of the prime movers in shooting down attempts in the early 1970s to unite the Church of England with the Methodists. As later, over women, so on this occasion Graham Leonard used his ammunition in support of a blunt restatement of the traditions of the Anglican Church.

Progressing to the diocese of Truro in Cornwall, he made his mark on the international stage in the 1978 Lambeth Conference, with a damning indictment of the ordination of women in several of the Anglican provinces. That opposition cost him his chances of Canterbury in 1980, or so his supporters have claimed.

Since his entry into the House of Lords as Bishop of Truro, Graham Leonard has used his inbuilt and obvious conservatism and hence acceptability to the government benches to persuade them to modify some of their legislative schemes – most notably in the field of education. Again he has swayed debates with the sheer depth of his knowledge and his preparation, and with the logic which he has displayed when on his feet:

> Because of the opportunities offered by my membership of the House of Lords, for example, the prominent part [allotted to him in matters political] is given by the media rather than sought. Though I do believe that if we are called upon to be involved in such issues there is no point in doing it half-heartedly. In my involvement in such affairs, I have been concerned to advocate and work for what can be done or prevented within the limits of legislation to enable any legislation to take account of and reflect the true nature of man.

A donnish, rather saintly man who is never more at ease than when at home with his family and pets, Graham Leonard perpetually has the air of one forced reluctantly into the limelight. It would be a mistake though to see him as a one-issue prophet, standing and falling by his position on women's ordination. He has spoken out on a whole range of moral issues, challenging the vacillations and agreement to differ of his fellow bishops on such matters as divorce, remarriage and homosexuality.

Prophets

If David Jenkins's prophetic qualities appear in his being a man
ahead of his time and ahead of the majority of his church, then
Graham Leonard is a prophet standing out against time, against the
mores and the moods of today – the Archbishop Lefebvre of his
church, as one commentator put it, in a reference to the excommunicated ultra-traditionalist French prelate who has rubbished the
modern age of the Catholic church. Whether Graham Leonard will,
over the issue of women priests, ultimately go, or be forced to go, as
far as Lefebvre in setting up his own sect, a church within a church,
remains to be seen.

8

Pastors and Peacemakers

———

The biblical image of the leaders of the church as pastors is a recurring one. The metaphor of God the shepherd and his people the sheep, protected and fed by him, runs throughout the Old and New Testaments. It finds its most eloquent and detailed analysis in St John's gospel with Jesus's parable, 'I am the good shepherd, I know my own, and they know me.'

Far be it from us to criticize the Holy Spirit's choice of metaphor, but perhaps we could be forgiven for worrying about the contemporary relevance of the shepherd role model. After all, how many shepherds have you seen in action? Moreover, exactly why are the shepherds so concerned for their sheep? What happens to the sheep once they have been fattened for market? It is not too difficult to know your own sheep when they have a huge brandmark all over them. Nor is it difficult to feed them in the British Isles. Grass may have been thin on the ground of Middle Eastern deserts, but the problem nowadays in this part of the world is to stop the sheep from feeding on other people's grass.

From our personal experience of interviewing bishops for this book, however, we have to report that any criticism of the shepherd/sheep metaphor is regarded as tantamount to heresy. (Likewise any irreverent use of it, as in suggesting that shepherds should not live in big farmhouses.) Our worries about this are not, however, entirely frivolous. Christ's parables were designed for his audience of shepherd folk. Would he have continued to talk about shepherds and sheep to those whose twentieth-century faith has to be nurtured in the inner city? All the bishops' roles involve communication with their people. We have already criticized the bishops for talking in too technical a language about such problems as contraception and *in vitro* fertilization. We would merely add a note of caution while on the theme of bishops as pastors to the effect that, while we welcome simple language and analogies, the bishops should from time to time pause to consider whether the metaphors are conveying the message properly.

A more contemporary image of the bishop is that of the peacemaker. As suggested in the previous chapter on prophets, the practical circumstances of the diocese that the bishop heads can be the most important factor in how he approaches his task. The pastor in the comfortable diocese on the south coast of England can be almost indistinguishable from the peacemaker on the streets of Belfast. What is different is their context, the area where they operate. Their actions and words as bishops can often be very similar, or at least based on closely related concepts.

Just as the idea of pastor is a strong one in the Bible, so too is that of peacemaker. 'Blessed are the peacemakers, they shall be called the children of God' (Matthew 5, 3). In its simplest and best-known form in the Sermon on the Mount, this essential part of Jesus's teaching to his followers was the imperative to be bringers of peace. His ministry of reconciliation stood on a par with that of being a shepherd to his flock.

Westminster

The scriptural texts on the pastoral role shape the perception of Cardinal Basil Hume as to what a bishop should be:

A bishop is first of all a pastor. The Latin derivation of that word says a great deal, I think, because a pastor is a shepherd. So the model of the bishop will always be the Good Shepherd as is depicted in John. And then there is the background in that chapter and in the book of Ezekiel which contrasts the good with the bad shepherd. So when you come down to it Our Lord said, 'Feed my sheep'. He said to Peter in John's gospel, 'Do you love me more than these others?' This was a mandate that was given to Peter, and the mandate that is given to all successors of the apostles – to feed my sheep.

But as both Cardinal Archbishop of Westminster and leader of the Catholic community in England and Wales (Scotland has its own set-up) Basil Hume often has conflicting impulses as to where to direct his pastoral care, and quite who are his sheep.

When I arrived in London there were those who said don't bother about the diocese, leave that to other people, you've got to be a national figure. Then there were others who said for God's sake don't forget that you're the bishop of a diocese. Now which voice was I to listen to? My answer is that I haven't decided yet. Perhaps I've fallen between two stools.

It could be argued that since arriving, unexpectedly, at the palatial and unwieldy Archbishop's House in Westminster from the North Yorkshire abbey of Ampleforth where he had been head of a Benedictine community, Basil Hume has managed rather successfully to balance the conflicting pulls on his time. Although he'd be too modest to admit it, the division of his large diocese into four areas, each with a bishop in charge, has resulted in more effective pastoral care with the bulk of parish visitations and the like taken off his already crowded schedule. 'I've told my auxiliaries – you must run your areas as if they are independent dioceses – and that they do, although we come together once a week to keep in touch.'

Basil Hume none the less maintains an active pastor's role in his diocese. When his schedule permits it, he hosts days of recollection and reflection for the local homeless – a problem that he has been very concerned about since his elevation:

If I weren't in this job, and if I weren't a monk, I should like to do something like run Centrepoint [a central London hostel for the homeless]. I feel very deeply about young people pouring into London at risk. I say constantly this is where the church should be, this is our job. Where would St Vincent de Paul have been today? Round about Centrepoint.

His concern for the homeless demonstrates well Basil Hume's dual role as a pastor. Not only does he seek to help them back to their feet, but as a national leader he attempts to direct the community's attention to the plight of such marginalized groups:

When you come to caring for the flock, then you've got to have a special concern for the disadvantaged, for the poor, for those who are not able to care for themselves. Once you begin to make the flock your special concern, then of course how they fare in the world, their condition, becomes a matter of rather considerable importance. Anything that is a denial of respect for their persons, or any injustice in their situation, that will call for the involvement of the pastor – so it is in that way that we also get involved in matters which are also the concern of the politician.

And as leader of the Catholic community, Basil Hume is bound to be pushed into the position of being a statesman, concerned with the well-being of the nation and its morality. This is a pastoral concern that he undertakes largely without denominational basis:

> Although one fights hard against being told that one is the leader of the 6 million Catholics in this country, there is a sense in which you are the only cardinal. And if you have that role, a spiritual leadership role within the nation, then you're bound I suppose to be considered as having some relevance to the rest of the nation. As the Chief Rabbi does.

However, whereas the Chief Rabbi has very clearly identified himself with one particular section of the political spectrum – and has received a peerage from Mrs Thatcher for his trouble – Basil Hume has remained aloof from the hurly-burly of party politics in the eyes of the public. This is partly explained by his saintly demeanour; whenever he appears on television or radio he carries with him the distinct aura of holiness.

It is also explained by a careful and intelligent interpretation of his national role as a pastor. When he has intervened in matters of state, he has taken his stand unequivocally on the grounds of justice and morality. In addition, his spirituality is used to advantage: he backs humbly into the limelight – as one commentator once put it – the simple monk dragged reluctantly into a world obsessed with material concerns: 'I think that there is a facet in which Ministers think that the spiritual life is important. Whenever I'm asked to go and talk in the City, I always say to them I presume you want me to talk about my thing, since I know nothing about your thing.' But Basil Hume has never been a simple monk. A highly intelligent, complex character, he spent much of his life in the monastery at Ampleforth, noted for its wealth, influence and scholastic tradition.

Yet the Cardinal has a great gift for putting himself on the level of ordinary people, as when he told a BBC sports reporter in 1986 that he'd like the *Match of the Day* theme played at his funeral to commemorate the many childhood hours he spent on the terraces of Newcastle United in his home town; or when he revealed to a women's magazine in 1981 that it would be 'marvellous' to have a wife. (*Debrett* in May 1988 granted him this wish in their *Distinguished People of Today* which listed the Cardinal as having married one Lady Bridget Mullens. He took the printing error in fine form – 'marriages can take place by proxy, but this is going a bit far.')

One senior Labour MP once described Basil Hume as more establishment than the establishment, the senior churchman that politicians most respected. David Owen is another who has paid tribute to the moral and spiritual guidance the Cardinal offers. Indeed he comes from a very establishment background. His father, a prominent surgeon, was a knight. His mother was French, and his sister married the Cabinet Secretary, Lord Hunt. Observers have noted a distinct unwillingness on Basil Hume's part to knock the establishment. In contrast to his predecessor, Cardinal Heenan, who came from a very humble background and was often to be heard attacking those in positions of power, Basil Hume has preferred guarded, coded and generalized criticisms that have been overshadowed by the more specific, up-front and vocal cries of the Anglican bishops. It is his impossible desire for 'clear, incisive, challenging, yet non-controversial' statements, as one former colleague noted, that has made him the politicians' friend.

His guidance to Ministers would be of a specific kind – lobbying, for example, on behalf of the homeless, or those convicted, unjustly he feels, of the Guildford pub bombings. The wide-ranging and public denunciations of government policy that have been issued by Anglican bishops have not been heard from the Cardinal, opening him to the charge of having a limited perception of the role of a pastor, concentrating on the marginalized to the exclusion of a broader-based community.

If he is not at his happiest in a political role, we asked him, what is it about his job that he most enjoys? His answer showed how he values his pastoral work:

> I think that the thing that really meant a great deal to me in recent history was when, organized by Mother Teresa's nuns, I gave a half-day recollection with the ladies and gentlemen who would have been sleeping rough that night in Westminster. We

wandered around the cathedral together, doing the stations of the cross. I think what's wonderful about being a bishop is that you can chat with anyone. You can chat with guys who are drinking on the piazza. I don't find any difficulty there. I find myself almost at home in that world. The most marvellous thing about being a bishop is that small gestures can go a long, long way and that is the most rewarding thing about it. Shaking someone's hand in the street, shaking all the hands in the parish after Mass, where you can only give each person fifteen seconds. I have a great principle that when I'm in a parish hall, I make a point of shaking every single hand. I make a point of looking that person straight in the eye, and I try consciously for fifteen seconds to make sure that that person is the only person that matters. It's quite tiring and you don't succeed the way you should.

But what, cynics may ask, is distinctive about a bishop doing this, rather than a social worker? The answer lies in the spiritual dimension of the bishop's pastoral role, well illustrated by Cardinal Hume's own life. Cardinal Hume cuts a mystical figure, the Holy Monk, a patently spiritual man of God. When he celebrates the Mass he seems to be in a trance, head bowed down to the altar, almost oblivious of the outside world, a man at one with God.

A bishop must be a man of prayer, a holy man. Thus there was great symbolism in the way in which the leading bishops of Europe celebrated the 1,500th anniversary of the birth of St Benedict. They went on a pilgrimage to the Abbey of St Scholastica (Benedict's sister) in Subiaco in Italy on 28 September 1980, led by a Benedictine monk and bishop, Cardinal Hume. Cardinal Hume's sermon emphasized the happy coincidence that the anniversary happened to fall in the middle of a Synod of bishops in Rome, which enabled many bishops from around the world to join him on the pilgrimage:

> The interests and concerns of the bishops of one continent are shared today, and indeed always, by the bishops of other lands. We, the bishops of Europe, are one with our brethren, and with what concerns them. Such mutual collaboration, expressing the idea of the co-responsibility of the whole college of bishops for the life of the church in every part of the world, is

one of the main characteristics of the ecclesiology of the Second Vatican Council.

The Cardinal proceeded to stress the pilgrim vision of the episcopal role:

> Life is a pilgrimage out of the valley of man's depressed state to the heights of the hills where, as was the case with Moses, the glory of God can be seen. Bishops, with their priests, are spiritual leaders on that journey. St Benedict can advise us on how we should be, for he has much to say on spiritual leadership.

Perhaps St Benedict gives a clue to this spiritual dimension we expect from our bishops. Although St Benedict himself was not a bishop, he was twice an abbot, who has a similar status within the church. As the Cardinal said of St Benedict,

> He gathered ordinary people around him. Men and women came together in community and followed his Rule in their own monasteries as they still do today. He gave them a new way of looking at life, precisely because they were to learn to put God at the very centre of their lives. That is the key for all of us.

St Gregory tells us that Benedict lived as he had written. He was a wise, moderate and compassionate abbot. He was truly what the word abbot literally means, a father, just as a bishop should be. But he achieved his spiritual peace above all through prayer. Prayer clearly plays a vital part in the life of a monastery and of a monk and the dedication to living the gospel, living in a Christ-like way, is obviously also crucial. But how can the Rule of St Benedict, or the example of St Benedict himself, be applied to the rest of the non-monastic world, including our bishops? Well, it should be remembered that St Benedict was not a priest but a layman. Most of his monks were not ordained either, so he was not writing for priests. His Rule was written originally to help groups of Christians to unite in their search for God and to support and encourage each other in so doing. Seen in that light, there is nothing strange in suggesting that bishops need above all to be praying priests, to be holy people.

We would argue that some such element of holiness or spirituality is a vital ingredient in the character of a bishop before he is truly believable. We do not want bishops who can be confused with manipulating bureaucrats, 'Sir Humphreys'. We do not want our bishops to be confused with politicians, 'David Owens' – quasi-establishment figures of opposition, crying in the wilderness. We do not want our bishops to be merely slick media performers, 'Terry Wogans'. We want them, on the contrary, to be signs of contradiction. We want them to represent, in their own lives, a challenge to temporal, materialistic values. We know that they cannot be exactly Christ-like since they are fallible human beings. But we would like them to try. We like the idea that our bishops are in closer contact with God. That they are leading us, as pastors, on a pilgrimage towards a deeper understanding of life.

Basil Hume has been playing such a pastor's role not only in England but also on a European, ecumenical stage for many years, dating back to before his appointment as Archbishop of Westminster in 1976. As Abbot of Ampleforth since 1963 he had become a noted ecumenist, travelling widely to theologians' and bishops' meetings on the subject. On the day of his installation at Westminster he led a group of Benedictine monks down to Westminster Abbey to sing vespers, the first time this had happened since the Reformation (Westminster Abbey having previously been a Benedictine abbey). It was a clear signal of his ecumenical concern, which has been followed by addresses to the Church of England General Synod in 1978 (the first cardinal to give one) and by a central role in the Pope's 1982 visit to Britain, and his landmark trip to Canterbury cathedral. 'I believe that relationships between the churches can never be the same again after that ceremony,' the Cardinal has remarked.

Canterbury

Although Basil Hume has become a familiar figure in Europe as President of the Council of European Bishops' Conferences, his international profile outside the rather narrow confines of Western Europe is not high, making speculative talk of his candidacy for the papacy ill-founded. Robert Runcie, the Cardinal's counterpart as a national church leader in England, has by contrast a clear world-wide role as Archbishop of Canterbury as titular head of the global

Anglican communion. It is that duality between domestic and international that is the essential contrast between Robert Runcie and Basil Hume as pastors – not the status afforded to the Archbishop as primate of the established Church of England.

The role of Archbishop of Canterbury in global terms is ill-defined. It is perhaps easier to say what he is not. He is not a pope – and Dr Runcie himself has made plain his unwillingness to be seen in such a light on many occasions, including in his opening address at the 1988 Lambeth Conference.

> We have no intention of developing an alternative papacy . . . I for one would want their provisional character [of the links binding the various Anglican provinces] made absolutely clear; like tents in the desert, they should be capable of being easily dismantled when it is time for a pilgrim people to move on.

Such freedom to develop in different areas of the globe the concept of a pilgrim people is a good idea in theory – but not one that the history of the Anglican communion would bear out. In his address Robert Runcie was speaking almost as if he were a global pastor in title alone. By describing the relationship between the provinces of the Anglican communion he heads as essentially transitory, he was *de facto* abdicating the practical leadership role assumed by his predecessors as Archbishop of Canterbury. The office has, of course, carried with it little formal authority over the international church, but is rather like the position of a constitutional monarch – with rights to guide, encourage and warn. Previous archbishops have used them to good effect to stamp their authority on the Anglican communion. The very fact that Robert Runcie was giving the keynote opening address at Lambeth is evidence enough of their legacy. As an international pastor, however, Runcie has lacked both the will and the sort of dominant personality necessary to follow in the footsteps of men like Michael Ramsey in asserting his authority and leadership on such issues as ecumenical initiatives.

But then such a judgement is not entirely fair to Dr Runcie, for his tenure of the see of Canterbury has coincided with the collapse of the communion into crisis over women priests and bishops, as we have seen in an earlier chapter. His success or otherwise as a pastor will be judged on how effectively he handles this issue, on how effectively he can combine being pastor and peacemaker, and what sort of world-wide Anglican church emerges.

Thus far Robert Runcie has not performed with any great conviction. He has announced his own conversion – somewhat tardy and rather lukewarm, sceptics would say – to the idea of women priests. But he has also hinted that in his heart of hearts he cannot see his flock in England being won over by the arguments in favour. His contributions to debates in Synod have not been of sufficient calibre or passion to win over waverers.

There in a nutshell is the problem of his office. What is good for the Anglican communion is not necessarily right for the Church of England. As head of both, which way does he turn? Robert Runcie has tried to turn both ways, opening him to criticisms well summed up by one newspaper commentator who suggested that the Archbishop might be better off writing leaders for the *Guardian*.

The question of a woman's place in the Anglican communion has highlighted the impossible task facing the Archbishop of Canterbury as pastor to two flocks. In effect Robert Runcie is being asked to choose: fall in with the more go-ahead provinces of Canada, America, New Zealand and Ireland and ordain women in England and thus preserve unchanged the unity of the whole Anglican church under the titular authority of Canterbury, but risk splitting the Church of England in the process; or protect his English base and avoid making a decision on ordination, and thus face a rebellion on the international stage. Robert Runcie has tried to have the best of both worlds, slowly paving the way for an eventual concession to women in the Church of England, while endlessly delaying the decision in the world-wide arena by reference to committees.

Before the 1988 Lambeth Conference there was much talk of the break-up of the Anglican communion. It is to Dr Runcie's credit as a diligent pastor that he prevented this. But he has merely postponed the problems. A decision has to be taken, the pastor has to give a lead, and he has not. This has left him vulnerable to attack from both sides of the debate. He has been accused of nailing his colours to the fence, of exceeding his own theological and intellectual capacity by rising without trace to Canterbury, and, in a memorable gibe from Clive James, of being 'the man to hire if what you want at your wedding is platitudes served up like peeled walnuts in chocolate syrup.'

Yet all these judgements ignore Robert Runcie's very real

attempts to update and realign the office he holds to take account of rapidly changing circumstances. His biographer, Margaret Duggan, described his personal standpoint as 'a moderate Catholic inclined towards radical views, though occasionally more conservative – as in the matter of the ordination of women – than might have been expected'. These qualities of being a man acceptable to many shades of opinion are undoubtedly the ones that commended him as Archbishop in the first place. However, Dr Runcie's talk of accepting a universal primacy of the Pope in a reunited Christian church, as well as his trip to the Vatican in 1989, has alienated the more protestant wing of his own church.

He has also taken his pastoral duties seriously – travelling widely, surrounding himself with able lieutenants who have freed him from the vast administrative and bureaucratic burden that is part and parcel of his tenancy of Lambeth Palace. He has taken seriously his diocesan responsibilities, trying to spend as many weekends as possible at the Old Palace, his official residence in Canterbury, despite his wife's reported dislike of the house.

As a national pastor he stressed in an interview soon after his appointment in 1980 that he would avoid 'the hollowness of ringing declarations and general moralizing divorced from a direct experience of the doubts and difficulties of ordinary people'. And he has not been afraid to speak up for those ordinary people, as we have detailed already in his dealings with the government over the inner cities and over the Falklands memorial service.

York

Like the other pastors described in this chapter, Robert Runcie has a gift for seeming like a good chap to the public. He is not the austere scholar that a prophet like the Bishop of Durham often seems to be. Neither is he as remote as his second-in-command, John Habgood in York. Robert Runcie's sense of humour and his ability to laugh at himself – as when he told Sue Lawley on 'Desert Island Discs' that he had first become interested in the church at the age of eleven in order to pursue a pretty girl called Betty who was a pupil in a Sunday School in his native Crosby – undoubtedly endear him to the nation as a pastor. As he commented on one occasion: 'We have nothing to contribute to building a better world unless we speak in a simple and human way from the heart of contradiction.' However, it would seem that the very contradictions that show up that human side are also the ones that make Robert Runcie's task as a pastor an almost impossible one – he has failed to reconcile the conflicting calls of his office at a time of crisis.

Where Robert Runcie has tried to operate as a pastor and a peacemaker on the international stage of the Anglican communion, it has been John Habgood who has taken up that mantle in the confines of the Church of England. A distant and frosty character by nature, the Archbishop of York, the second most senior figure in the Church of England, does not possess the necessary qualities in a media-conscious age to take on the national pastoral role as do Cardinal Hume and Archbishop Runcie. He lacks their ability to appear relaxed in the public eye, and is happier in the confines of the many committees and bureaucracies that lie behind the facade of the Church of England's central London headquarters, Church House.

It is in these behind-the-scenes situations that John Habgood is at his most effective as a peacemaker, and it is in that capacity that he epitomizes the bureaucratic bishop. The current crisis and disunity in the Church of England has provided him with the opportunity. A peacemaker was needed, and he possessed both the authority and the status, as Archbishop of York, and the dedication to detail, and to discussion and debate, to take on the task. 'Church administration can take you into a funny little world. It teaches you about sin and other things ... so in that sense you don't get cut off. You learn a good deal about human nature.'

As Bishop of Durham for ten years, and since 1983 as head of the second-ranking see in the Church of England, John Habgood has cut quite a swathe as an efficient, some would say brilliant, administrator. But that managing-director-like approach stretches beyond his own diocese and Church House, to embrace the General Synod of the Church of England where John Habgood has often played the role as a focus of unity in difficult and divisive times, particularly on the women-priests issue:

The bishop is a managing, leading figure in a fairly large, complex organization which is very widespread. Part of the

153

national role of a bishop is of course being a member of the House of Bishops in the synodical structure. Bishops tend to play quite a prominent part in the debate at Synod.

Indeed it has been in these twice-yearly meetings of the Church of England that John Habgood has been seen at his most effective as a peacemaker and reconciler. He is a very fluent speaker and a persuasive chairman of debates. He appears very much at home in the environment of a debating chamber, and among his achievements has been the successful piloting through of the Alternative Service Book despite the vocal protests of those who felt that nothing could better the Book of Common Prayer.

An austere man in his early sixties with an academic background as a scientist (Eton and King's College, Cambridge), John Habgood belongs to that section of the leadership of the Church of England that Gary Bennett dubbed the 'liberal ascendancy' in his controversial *Crockford's* preface. While Bennett meant that as a smear against the Archbishop, the element of truth that there was in the charge demonstrates rather the strength of John Habgood as a peacemaker. For while Bennett saw the centre ground, theologically speaking, of the Church of England as possessing a distinct ideology, in reality it operates rather more as a curb on the excesses of both Evangelical and high-church wings – as a uniting force. John Habgood's own entry into the Church of England was as a fervent Evangelical, but as one commentator puts it, 'he was far too sensible to keep that up for long.'

Possibly the best brain in the Church of England, according to his colleagues, the Archbishop is certainly clear-thinking enough to realize that for one in his senior position it is a mistake to be seen as identifying too definitely with any cause or partisan viewpoint. His predecessor as Bishop of Durham, the late Ian Ramsey, had a phrase that well highlights John Habgood's approach – 'certainty in religion, tentativeness in theology'.

But that ability to respect both sides of the argument, to encourage others to work to find their mutual ground, has earned John Habgood few admirers. In part this is because people dislike those who persuade them to compromise, but it springs mainly from the general impression of the Archbishop's peacemaking role as something equivalent to a head boy's imperiousness. In a church that puts great store by social niceties, John Habgood is a cold fish, detached, lacking in small talk, and not a man to suffer fools gladly. His friends describe him as in private quite the opposite, a judgement that his hobby of mending children's toys would seem to bear out.

He is thought to have a close working relationship with Robert Runcie and David Jenkins, although his approach to being a bishop is rather different. Where the press and the church are often reluctant to attack Dr Runcie as its leader, they pick off John Habgood as an easy target. A whispering campaign is already under way in Anglican circles under the slogan A B H – Anyone But Habgood – referring to the forthcoming vacancy at Canterbury.

By and large the Archbishop ignores such currents – rather disdainfully. But just occasionally his patience and peaceful intent breaks, as when for instance he launched a fierce attack on the author of the *Crockford's* preface that was so scathing about Dr Runcie and himself. Although it is not clear if John Habgood knew that Gary Bennett's was the hand behind the piece, prominent Anglicans have publicly attacked the Archbishop's uncharacteristic outburst, which did nothing to allay the tragic sequence of events that culminated in Mr Bennett's suicide.

Truer to his character is another aspect of John Habgood's work, and one that is mostly overlooked by his detractors, his commitment to reconciliation between the churches. As the senior Anglican on the British Council of Churches, a body which unites all the denominations save the Catholics, he has progressively broadened the approach of the organization, and this year it is hoped that the Catholics will finally agree to join its revised structures. On an international plane too, John Habgood is a familiar face at the Geneva-based World Council of Churches.

However, despite such unsung work, many commentators are now convinced that John Habgood will miss out on Canterbury. His own brand of being a peacemaker, a reconciler, is considered too low key, too cautious at a time when the Church of England and the Anglican communion are in need of a commanding figure to heal their wounds. The Archbishop of York is seen rather as a bureaucratic bishop.

Brighton

What is around him, as indicated at the start of this chapter, plays a large part in shaping a bishop's approach to his office. Because of the demands of their national role, the three other figures in this chapter are not able to operate purely as diocesan pastors. Cormac Murphy-O'Connor, by contrast, has for over a decade headed the decidedly affluent south-coast Catholic diocese of Arundel and Brighton. This shepherd has been able to concentrate his efforts on his flock and has been guided by a determination to meet them on their own terms, wherever they are. He would point to high levels of homelessness in the urban areas of Brighton, and to the damage caused to a whole twenty- to forty-year-old Sussex and Surrey generation by the 'rather ruthless, acquisitive Thatcherite society', but much of his diocese fits easily into the gin and golf, vodka and Volvo stereotype of retired army personnel and wealthy accountants:

> In the Pope's first encyclical, *Redemptoris Hominis*, what he is saying was that people are led to the way of Christ by the way of man. In other words you don't actually start with God in today's society, you start with man. It's from the experiences of life, community, that you realize there's a mystery and that the mystery is one of spirit and love, and of God. The church has to find new ways of evangelizing, speaking and getting through to people.

And as head of his diocese since 1977, Cormac Murphy-O'Connor has been searching for those ways. His starting point is that the church must be firmly rooted in the culture that is around it in order to have any power in people's lives. It is not a question of adapting teaching to make it more comfortable, less challenging, but rather of finding effective ways to reach his flock in a secular age:

> The secularity of our society makes it extraordinarily likely that young Catholics will not practise their faith. So what are we going to do about that? We are going to have to enable them to lead their faith in ways where they will be both nourished by it and understand what it is to have a life of faith.

But if Cormac Murphy-O'Connor has continually exhibited a certain independence of the current Roman ruling sect in his determination to bring the church to the people of his wealthy and worldly-wise diocese, it is an independence that he sees as firmly rooted in the traditions of the Catholic church:

> I suppose the great word is apostolic tradition – if the early church which had oversight was given to the apostles, then who now is to hold together God's word, lived out in history? That seems to me to be the task of the bishops – why they've got to rule and guide and teach.

The teaching part of his work as pastor is an important part of Cormac Murphy-O'Connor's work and it is a commitment that has carried him outside his diocese. He has given a strong lead in ecumenism – especially in the field of Anglican–Catholic relations in his role as co-chairman of the second Anglican Roman Catholic Commission which is investigating the background to a closer agreement between the two churches. He is spoken about in Anglican circles as the human face of the Catholic church, a tribute again to his work as a pastor in dealing with people in the situation in which they are – not where he'd like them to be.

Occasionally though, his determination to be a teacher and to be with his people can lead him into difficulties. In his insistence on planning for the future of the church, re-evangelizing for the next century, he runs the risk of being too innovative for the liking of some of his people or some of his superiors in Rome. This shows the way in which a bishop who sees prophecy and pastoral work as inextricably linked will never rest content. He must integrate the different aspects of his work. He must challenge his followers, even if they are thereby troubled, otherwise he is not really caring for them.

9

Wider Visions

―――――

In the last two chapters we have travelled from Durham to Brighton, from prophets to pastors. Where do we go to now? That is, after all, the question which we feel the churches in England should be answering before they start naming the names of their next leaders.

If we may borrow and adapt the metaphor used by the Liverpudlian bishops, we feel the need for a journey outwards before the inward journey can be completed. Let us look at the role of bishops elsewhere before we settle on a vision for the English churches.

Belfast

We do not have to travel very far for a sense of perspective. Northern England's bishops might be living in a different world, but in a religious sense Belfast is perhaps closer to Liverpool than Brighton is. What happens in Ireland, north and south, is of the greatest concern to bishops in England. The work of bishops across the Irish Sea ought also to be of interest. Are the bishops in Northern Ireland part of the problem, or the solution, or both? Does their dramatic role as peacemakers have any lessons for their English counterparts?

As we have seen in the previous two chapters, a bishop's role is often determined by the place, the town in which he finds himself. In the case of Bishop Cahal Daly, whose diocese of Down and Connor centres on the city of Belfast, the need to be a reconciler was immediately apparent.

What better text could there be for a bishop in Northern Ireland than St Paul's letters to the church at Ephesus where he talks of Christ being the one who 'has made the two into one and broken down the barrier which used to keep them apart'.

Cahal Daly cannot claim in his seven years at the head of one of the world's most turbulent dioceses to have torn down the metaphysical Berlin Wall that separates the Catholic and Protestant areas of west Belfast. But he has given a clear lead in working to break down the mistrust, hostility and hatred that have historically divided the communities there. As well as preaching the church's message of reconciliation, not revenge, of progress through justice not violence, the bishop has gone out of his way to make himself a visible symbol of peace, most notably by officiating at the funerals of every one of the innocent Catholic victims of sectarian violence:

> It was a conscious decision. No two funerals are ever the same. One never gets used to it – the grief and the desolation expressed. I have visited all the homes of the bereaved and have been at forty-one funerals in these past seven years. That for me has been an horrific experience. Sometimes I cannot keep back the tears and I simply sit and weep with the widow and family.

Whatever his private feelings of grief, and despite speaking in his funeral homilies of a sentiment of 'near despair and helplessness at the evil forces that have been released within our community', Cahal Daly has never on these most public of occasions wavered from a constant message of peace. With the eyes of Northern Ireland, Britain and the international community on him, he has repeatedly condemned the men of violence on both sides, disowned the IRA and its murderous campaign, and urged his flock and his listeners towards coexistence and greater understanding.

It is a message, the Bishop feels, that strikes a chord in the community despite the ever increasing number of civilian deaths: 'At these funerals I feel my faith strengthened by the bereaved family's faith. My hope for my country to be at peace is enhanced by the forgiveness of these people. I have never once been aware of sentiments of retribution or retaliation.'

Despite the almost universal high esteem in which this bishop is held by his clergy, some of his flock living in the heart of west Belfast disagree with him in this final observation. They have told us that the Bishop is an outsider who has spent much of his life in academic institutions, and that his view of west Belfast from

Bishop's House in the genteel surburbs of north Belfast is naïve.

But truth is that a few of Cahal Daly's flock are bitterly opposed to him because he does *not* support the men of violence. Some hard-line republicans make a point of abusing him when he visits their parishes. They like to claim that he does not understand. But he understands only too well. Nevertheless, what does he make of the point that bishops are not seen often enough on the streets with their people? It is a charge that Cahal Daly rebuts with characteristic directness:

> One of the crosses of my life as a bishop is the difficulty of reconciling my desire and need to be out with the people as their pastor, and to be working at my desk, reminding society, challenging the wealthy with their responsibility for the struggling in society. It is a tension that I've never been able to bring into harmony.

And indeed while priests work on a parish or district basis, Cahal Daly, because of the situation in Belfast, has attracted a national and international audience. Despite being almost at pensionable age when he was named as Bishop of Down and Connor, and ignoring ill-health that has brought him one major heart attack already, Cahal Daly has been a ceaseless peacemaker and leader at many different levels. His time to be with his people on the streets of Belfast is necessarily limited by the need to lobby for them in a wider world.

One of the marks of Cahal Daly's success as a peacemaker has been his ability to work closely with, and at the same time challenge, the various institutions of the state in the north of Ireland which had hitherto been shunned by the Catholic church and its people. For example his relations with the Royal Ulster Constabulary include a close working arrangement with Sir John Hermon, who retired as Chief Constable in 1989. Even in the darkest moments for the force, as when it was accused of operating a shoot-to-kill policy in the early 1980s, or when its officers saw their homes fire-bombed by angry Loyalist mobs in 1986, Cahal Daly has continued working to make both the RUC and the Catholic community aware of the need to grow in understanding of each other. He has called for Catholics to join the RUC while at the same time unequivocally criticizing the police on numerous occasions. He has, in other words, helped initiate a dialogue:

Even though the RUC have made and are making very real efforts to become an impartial, professional police force, they have not yet succeeded in breaking down the suspicions and resentments of the nationalist community. They still have to live down a murky past. After all, we are only eighteen years away from the time when the police on the ground were siding with the Loyalist mobs against the Catholics.

His criticisms have always been constructive. His sustained campaign on behalf of six Irishmen convicted in 1975 of the Birmingham pub bombings has been based on the belief that the six are innocent and that their continued imprisonment postpones the day when the Catholic community in the north will have any faith in the fairness and impartiality of British justice. Without such faith, law and order cannot operate effectively.

Responding to that call for action from Pope Paul VI, who once described peace as not simply the absence of war, Cahal Daly has undertaken a long-running battle to build a secure economic and financial future for the Catholic community in west Belfast, an area blighted for many years with under-investment. In this campaign, the Bishop has dealt directly with the British government:

> There must be a close concern by bishops for justice, jobs and the structure of society – not in abstract principles but in concrete living. A pastor knows how his people are living and suffering. In that sense the bishop has to be the conscience of the people in power. But unless our challenge is backed up by positive action such as the allocation of resources, financial and other, to provide some mini-models of the sort of community we want, our voices will be ignored. It is no good saying to the government this is what you should be doing in west Belfast unless we as a church are doing what we say the government should be.

One area where Cahal Daly has attracted much criticism in his work for peace has been in his lukewarm reception for the integrated school movement in Northern Ireland. He has been condemned for refusing to allow Catholic pupils at these non-denominational establishments to have official chaplains or to receive their First Holy Communion or to be confirmed in their parish church alongside children from the local Catholic school. They have separate services. The Bishop bases his objection not on a dismissal of the potential of integrated schools to promote progress towards peace, but because he believes Catholic schools carry out this function better. As he told us:

> In my experience, those Catholics who are firmly committed to ecumenicism are those formed in the Catholic school systems. Anyone deeply formed in the Catholic faith cannot but have a strong ecumenical dimension. My support or not of integrated schools shouldn't be taken as a mark of my support for cross-community reconciliation. It is not hypocritical of me not to support them. But it is my belief that to succeed in solid faith formation, religion cannot be corralled into religion periods, but must be part of the ethos of the whole school.

It is not difficult to criticize this statement. Firstly, in the past it would be true that those Catholics who were most firmly committed to ecumenicism, not to mention those who are least committed to ecumenicism, would have been formed in the Catholic school systems because there was no realistic alternative for Catholics. The whole point is that the integrated school movement is trying to develop another way. Second, religion *is* part of the ethos of the whole integrated school. It would become an even greater part of that ethos if the Bishop would appoint chaplains.

When we put these points to the Bishop and criticized his decision to 'segregate' children from integrated schools in their reception of the sacraments, he clarified his views for us. He stressed that integrated schools were a new development, that they were not all the same and did not speak with one voice, so that it was difficult to make decisions with regard to the movement as a whole. He accepted that the parents were people of goodwill. He hoped that they would accept that he is also acting with the best of intentions, trying to balance the needs of the schools for which he has responsibility with the needs of this new development.

Cahal Daly told us that he was not dogmatic about integrated schools. But he explained that the modern church sees formation of young people for the sacraments as a partnership between home, school and parish. It would be wrong to obliterate the differences between Catholic and integrated schools just so that children could receive the sacraments together. Indeed, non-Catholic parents who send their children to integrated schools might feel that such schools were being taken over by the Catholic church if the Catholic children received the sacraments in the same way. Bishop Daly said that he was searching for a way to recognize the distinctiveness of integrated schools with an appropriate service, whether of First Holy Communion or of Confirmation.

With this explanation, the Bishop's stance on integrated schools seems much more reasonable. It is in marked contrast to the attitude taken by some of his priests who become extremely hot under the dog-collar whenever integrated schools are mentioned. They are their own worst enemies, enabling hostile sections of the media to portray them as bigots and deflecting attention from the outstanding achievements of Catholic schools.

Their bishop, however, has a more measured view. In the long run, we can be sure that there will still be Catholic schools and many more integrated schools and that Bishop Daly will have found a way to harmonize the two. But, as we have said, for the foreseeable future the majority of children in Northern Ireland will still be educated in segregated schools. So it is even more important that integrity in the curriculum continues to be safeguarded. The Catholic schools' openness to the government's initiatives on Education for Mutual Understanding and Cultural Heritage constitutes a much more welcome sign of hope.

The power of the Catholic school movement, as well as the integrated school movement, has a major role to play in constructing a more hopeful future for Northern Ireland. It is perhaps these two qualities, power and hope, which surround discussion of the role of bishops in Northern Ireland. How much power do they have? What kind of power is it? Is there much hope that they can use any power they possess constructively towards making peace? We asked Cahal Daly about his power as a peacemaker. He replied:

I have no power and seek no power other than the gospel I preach and the willingness of the people to accept its teaching. Bishops' and priests' influence is very considerable because of the power of the gospel they preach. It has the power to liberate people. But it is not a power to say 'stop the violence', and it stops. It is much more subtle and slow-moving than that. But I do believe it is effective. The Catholic church has been the greatest stabilizing force of the past twenty years here in rebuilding a society of hope.

We are all too close to events in the north of Ireland to judge the Bishop's last claim. Whatever stability the church may have brought to the situation through its work for better economic and social conditions for the minority community, a fundamental instability remains and the conflict continues despite Cahal Daly's efforts.

Could the Bishop have done more? Should he have done less? When we looked at the English and Northern Irish bishops' interventions in the realm of politics, we saw that they have been criticized time and again for interfering in other people's business. Returning to the problems of Northern Ireland, this difficulty is highlighted. Bishop Daly cannot avoid criticism. He does not expect to avoid it, of course, and he knows full well that much of the criticism will be unjustified. But how does he draw the line between the work of a bishop and that of a politician, especially in his special circumstances?

The Bishop insists that he never has meetings with politicians. His role as a pastor, a peacemaker, is in facilitating dialogue between communities. Bishop Daly is on record as saying, 'I would be grossly failing in my duty as a Christian pastor if I were to adopt any political position.' He deplores the tendency of others to identify Catholics with republicanism, and with support for the violent methods of the IRA. But aren't we now back to politics? Our earlier argument, after all, is that since it is impossible to separate religion from everyday life and everyday life from politics, there must be some overlap between religion and politics. In Northern Ireland, where many more issues are regarded as of constitutional significance than would be the case in a more stable society, the overlapping area is obviously large. Bishop Daly is clearly sensitive to the criticism that the bishops should not take over the mantle of politicians. But when politicians seem incapable of much forward movement, inevitably bishops will be hard pressed to maintain their distance.

Nevertheless, the Bishop is insistent upon the importance of the 'perceptible distancing' of all the mainstream churches in Northern Ireland from what he calls 'political Unionism and political nationalism'. Bishop Daly's approach seems to be to pave the way for politicians by slowly trying to correct misunderstandings. He has emphasized that 'nationalism and Unionism must be mutually recognized as equally noble'. That means, of course, considerable movement on the part of many Unionists. But Bishop Daly also recognizes that nationalists must move from the simplistic view that the aspirations of Unionists are illegitimate because their forefathers arrived somewhat later than the ancestors of nationalists. Both sides have been in the area for much longer than any non-Indian has been in the USA. So the Bishop continues to stress the need to recognize the good faith and legitimacy of other traditions. He also rules out entirely the use of violence for political ends. It is by now a common refrain from Catholic pulpits all over Northern Ireland that whereas the IRA claim they are dying for the Irish people, it is the Irish people who are dying for the IRA.

The problems of Northern Ireland are evident from the fact that anybody who adopts these two positions (respecting Unionism and condemning republican violence) will himself be mistakenly condemned as a traitor to nationalism, as a tool of the British government and the security forces. Pastors and prophets are without honour in their own country (whatever the ultimate destiny of that country). But the Bishop is unrepentant, at least on these matters. He can and does say at the same time, 'without qualification, I certainly will endorse a Catholic's decision to join the RUC' and unequivocally condemn the security forces for their mistakes. His respect for Unionism is no 'sell-out'. It is linked with an unswerving demand for the recognition of nationalism as 'totally legitimate, totally legal, totally morally, legally and constitutionally acceptable, provided that, as it does, it rejects all recourse to violence'.

So we return to the questions: has he done enough, has he done too much? Our own view is that the Bishop commands belief from all those of goodwill. He has done the right kind of things, he has refrained from doing many wrong things which others have urged him to do. The pressures of his job are almost beyond belief. Yet in this most sensitive of dioceses there is a lesson for all bishops, including those who operate in more sedate surroundings. Cahal Daly commands respect because he is, even to the most jaundiced eye, transparently a man of God, a believer, a holy man. To maintain a Christian vision in the most trying of circumstances is only possible with a deep and growing faith. Such faith asks awkward questions of believers. It has some of the prophetic quality we associate with the Bishop of Durham. It challenges the bishop's flock. But it also draws strength from the pastoral reality of that flock. The church in England should be looking to the example of the bishops in Northern Ireland, not so much with sympathy for their brethren's plight as with a sense of awe at the way in which the most difficult of missions is being accomplished.

Armagh

What about the peacemaking efforts of Robert Eames (to give him his correct Christian name, although the press seems to favour the more chirpy Robin) with respect to the north of Ireland? In the shorthand of the conflict, he sits on the other side of the sectarian fence from Cahal Daly. As Primate of the Protestant Church of Ireland, he is seen as a key figure on the Unionist side. Yet he is also the head of a national, all-Ireland church (albeit a small one, claiming the nominal adherence of about 5 per cent of the Irish people). To that church Ireland is one province, while Robert Eames's diocese of Armagh straddles the 1922 border.

In his national role, Robert Eames claims an essentially happy coexistence of Protestants within a Catholic state based on Dublin. He admits to reservations about the degree of toleration over questions like the outlawing of abortion and divorce, both the subject of recent referenda in the Republic, but essentially his view on the theoretical desirability of a United Ireland would be rather different from that of Northern Irish Protestants, many of whom would rather die than succumb to 'Rome rule' via Dublin.

As a leader and a peacemaker in the north of Ireland, Robert Eames has to make difficult choices because of his broader role within Ireland:

I have to be prepared to let the side down for the sake of ecumenicism. I have been criticized for such actions, for having surrendered something. It's a tightrope you walk and you have to be careful, judicious and have a degree of courage.

Yet, like Cahal Daly, he has never been afraid to be with his people within the north of Ireland in their hour of need. 'I decided on taking office in 1986 that I couldn't be an austere primate figure, that I must be out amongst my people, giving then a lead.'

Robert Eames has officiated at his share of funerals in his four years as primate. 'I myself have buried fifty-nine murder victims – members of the Church of Ireland. You cannot be in close pastoral touch with people like that without realizing the price in purely human, personal terms.' But his position with regard to the Unionist population is very different from that of Cahal Daly with the nationalists. The Church of Ireland is just one of the Protestant churches that has members in the north of Ireland. It does not enjoy the monopoly of the Catholic church, and coexists on its side of the sectarian divide with the Presbyterians and more fundamentalist sects, as exemplified by the Reverend Ian Paisley.

However, as a peacemaker Robert Eames thinks that such fragmentation of the Protestant churches can be seen as a strength. It allows him to encourage a plurality of approaches amongst the Protestant people of the north. He is not tied to the Unionist cause, though many of its adherents are in his congregation. Indeed his role as Primate of All Ireland is a constant reminder of the unity of Ireland for many purposes.

Robert Eames is therefore a freer agent in the Northern Ireland situation than Cahal Daly, and he interprets that freedom as allowing him to make more sweeping initiatives, such as his recent suggestion that devolved government would give the Province a stronger sense of cross-community identity:

> Northern Ireland is in a political vacuum, and there is a crying need for a way forward. It has been left to the church to enunciate that way. I've tried to do that. Then somebody else must take up the ball and run with it. Party politicians for example.

Robert Eames the peacemaker in the north of Ireland context is concerned with broad brush strokes, sketching plans and ideas and leaving politicians to carry out the details. He sees himself also as absolutely apolitical, concerned only with balancing the pastoral needs of his flock in the north with those in the Republic. Increasingly in recent months his scope for the sort of involved work that Cahal Daly undertakes has been reduced by a growing involvement on the international stage as a peacemaker within the world-wide Anglican communion.

Although at the age of fifty-one very much the junior among the Anglican primates, Eames was entrusted in the wake of the 1988 Lambeth Conference with the keynote task of addressing the world-wide implications of the ordination of women priests and bishops in some provinces of the church. He was asked to suggest a way forward that would be acceptable to diametrically opposed sides.

The choice of Robert Eames for this commission rather than any of the more established leaders of the Anglican communion, who head more numerous provinces than the comparative backwater of the Church of Ireland, has led to speculation that he may be in line as the next Archbishop of Canterbury. Indeed there were persistent rumours at Lambeth amongst the delegates that when Dr Runcie retires in 1990, his place would be taken by someone from outside the Church of England. It is a suggestion that Robert Eames greets with an impenetrable smile. After all, personal ambition is not an attribute for a future church leader.

As in Northern Ireland, so in the Anglican communion, the key concept in Robert Eames's approach to being a peacemaker has been the notion of pluralism of ideas and concepts, living with diversity. Safe in the knowledge that his own province has been a showpiece for cohesiveness in recent times, over questions of doctrine at least, Robert Eames has been able to address the wider questions facing the Anglican communion without fear of contradiction at home.

His personality is the key to understanding his role as peacemaker in this context. He is not a man dogged by dogma. A talented administrator, with an easy and relaxed charm that comes across well on television, he affects none of the airs and graces of his office. Some critics have told us he goes too far in the opposite direction of pragmatism, looking for the lowest common denominator as the point of compromise. His only non-negotiable principle is the unity of the Anglican communion.

Robert Eames is confident that that unity will not be shattered over women priests:

> This is an exciting if very difficult time for Anglicanism. I don't think there will be schism. But in ten years' time the face of the Anglican episcopate is going to be very different. There will be

more women bishops – I expect a second soon in New Zealand, and then another in the United States. The world-wide communion must broaden itself by pushing the walls back. We need to ask what exactly does it mean to be a member of a twenty-seven-strong world family of churches.

One suggestion that Robert Eames has put forward for future harmony would be a looser federation of the Anglican provinces than exists at present. Then there might be a central secretariat, not necessarily based in Lambeth, maintaining the unity of different regions of the church as they go their own way concerning women priests.

Such an agreement to differ is at the heart of his recommendations in the Eames Report, the result of his post-Lambeth look at the women's ordination question, endorsed by the world-wide primates at a gathering in Cyprus in May 1989. Its central argument is typical of Robert Eames's flexibility:

> Both protagonists and antagonists of the ordination of women to the priesthood and episcopate should consider carefully what anomalies they are prepared to accept for the sake of unity. Both sides would have to acknowledge that the other's position might in the long run prove to be the mind of the church.

Critics allege that such equivocation is the hallmark of Robert Eames – nailing his colours to the fence. Yet as a peacemaker it is this kind of delphic language that may save the Anglican communion from disaster, and that is the job he has been allocated.

Indeed, evidence of Robert Eames's success in this task is already apparent. He is constantly sought out in his Armagh home and on the international platform for his advice on the affairs of different provinces of the church. At the time of our interview, he was besieged with requests from the world's media to explain his report on women priests. His door is always open, or as he puts it with a broad smile, 'We eat, drink and sleep women priests.' The kind of international secretariat that he feels may serve as a more effective uniting force than the Archbishop of Canterbury's titular position is already under way, unofficially at least, in Armagh.

Rome

Ireland has proved to be more directly relevant to the quest for a new Archbishop of Canterbury than some readers might have expected. It is possible that Archbishop Eames will become more than an outside role model. He could become the next Archbishop of Canterbury himself. More probably, he could take much of the international burden of the next Archbishop of Canterbury away from Lambeth by heading an international secretariat in Armagh.

Moving much further afield, is there anything for our bishops to learn from the giant figures who have an international role or reputation? How, for instance, does the Bishop of Rome see his mission? Although his flock technically extends no further than Rome, of which he is bishop, Pope John Paul II has a world-wide responsibility for 840 million Catholics – and the figure increases each year. The notion of himself as pastor to this enormous flock is one that he has been at pains to emphasize throughout his ten-year pontificate – by words and deeds.

Repeatedly on public occasions, and also in his written teachings and letters, John Paul has referred to himself by the title Pastor, in preference to Pope or Pontiff. The notion of ruler has been discarded in favour of the concept of teacher and nurturer. And in physical terms, John Paul II has already clocked up going on for forty overseas trips, circumnavigating the globe so often as to make even the most indefatigable traveller's head spin. And he has not concentrated solely on predominantly Catholic countries. The tiny, less than 1 per cent Catholic minorities of Sweden and the Scandinavian countries recently witnessed his pastor's concern for their spiritual well-being.

Only Russia and China have eluded the Pope as major countries where he has yet to kiss the tarmac – and the former seems increasingly likely to fall to his charms as *glasnost* modifies the official atheist attitude of the Kremlin. China will be a harder nut to crack, especially after the crushing of the pro-democracy demonstrations in Peking, with the Catholic church that remains loyal to Rome and the Pope's pastoral care having been systematically suppressed over a thirty-year period.

Even in Italy, this first non-native pontiff for several centuries has been assiduous in travelling to every corner of the peninsula to meet the adopted flock that commands a disproportionate share of his pastoral concern.

This ceaseless motion has derived from two main aims of Karol Wojtyla's papacy: to restore a visible unity to the affairs of his far-flung flock, and to re-establish and personally reiterate a certainty in teaching and matters of faith that he regarded as to some extent absent during the last but one pontificate, that of Paul VI (1963–78). Where the latter was prone to indecision and disliked leaving the Vatican for any length of time, John Paul II has carried his muscular and confident approach to Catholicism out to his flock with all the zeal of a missionary. His voice has been regularly heard in all five continents. What was previously a distant sound to the majority of the world's Catholics living in the Third World environments of the Philippines, South Korea, Latin America or southern Africa has become a reality. The church's teaching role has been personally restated by the Pope himself. He has broken the monopoly of Western Europe on the attention of the papacy in favour of the developing nations.

Central among the concerns that John Paul II has repeatedly stressed during his travels has been the need to obey the church's teaching on morality – on marriage, contraception and the like. But he has also dwelt at length on the church's social teaching, often in areas where the poverty of the mass of the people can make Catholicism a radical, even revolutionary, gospel. He has not been afraid to address the specific needs of the millions he has visited, as was seen when he condemned the Paraguayan dictatorship of General Alfredo Stroessner in 1988, just months before it was swept away by a military revolt. Yet, as a pastor, John Paul II has a Herculean task in caring for and guiding his flock. His visits are a once-in-a-lifetime experience for many nations, even the most devout such as Ireland, which he greeted in 1979.

And there is the difficulty of determining what guidance to give to so many disparate flocks. The theological debates of the Northern European Catholic church over the nature of dissent, for example, can hardly be addressed in the same terms as the fears of the still largely missionary flock of Africa. Yet he has attempted that task, particularly in his insistence on a single line on such matters as sexual morality. This Pope's obvious desire for a united Catholic world-wide family has caused him to override local variations.

This has laid him open to the charge that as a pastor he is interested only in instructing his people, not in listening to their needs and their views. However, such flexibility, it could be argued, is beyond any individual. The office of world-wide pastor is too much for one man, and he is thus reduced to broad brush strokes, the lowest common denominator. When you add, to the extent of the task facing him, John Paul II's own background and the effect of the formative years he spent in the unique circumstances of Poland – a deeply Catholic nation caught in the post-1945 firing line between capitalism and socialism – his difficulties are seen as still more acute.

Yet John Paul has carried out his aims of uniting and guiding the flock with a certain gusto. In his use of the jet engine and his openness to the whims of the modern media, he can be considered the first truly twentieth-century pope. His face has become as well-known as that of the presidents and prime ministers of major countries. But in reality, in guiding his world-wide flock, he has to rely largely on his local bishops. His policy in appointing these men is examined elsewhere in this book, but the general trend in his pontificate has been towards a growing and creeping centralization on Rome, at the expense of individual conferences of bishops. The bureaucracy of Rome has been used to support the Pope in striving for greater uniformity and many minor decisions now have to be referred back to the various Vatican congregations. One European bishop commented recently that if modern transport did not exist, and all papal directives had to be delivered by pack-horse across the Alps as in centuries gone by, Rome's rulings would be of much less interest to local churches.

But there is an element in the Roman Curia that is beyond the control of the Pope himself. Since the reforms of the Second Vatican Council and the various secretariats that it threw up to carry out the church's new missions, Vatican bureaucracy has grown out of all recognition (and its spiralling costs have plunged the Holy See into debt). It would take a superhuman effort for any one man to keep abreast of its every move and turn – the death after thirty-three days in office of Pope John Paul I can largely be attributed to the vast administrative burden that he was unable to shoulder. Pope John Paul II is rarely in a position to undertake such supervision. His travelling as well as his frequent use of encyclicals and personal meditations on such subjects as the role of women in the church reduces his capacity to check what his officials are doing in his name as a pastor. It is a measure of John Paul's achievement that he has managed largely to eclipse such fears by sheer force of personality. As a pastor his most shining qualities have been his charisma, his energy and his air of spirituality.

Salvador to South Africa

These qualities can be found, of course, in other bishops all over the world. Perhaps the bishop who most notably inspired belief, and inspired his flock of believers, in recent times was Oscar Romero, Archbishop of San Salvador, who was gunned down as he said Mass on 24 March 1980. In his three years as head of the Catholic church in civil-war-torn El Salvador, Oscar Romero took on the role of the voice of the voiceless, speaking out against the murderous activities of government supporters in killing their opponents and exploiting the poor. In a situation in which no one else was prepared to risk standing up and speaking out for peace and justice, Oscar Romero was fearless. In one of his final addresses he spoke of the need for bishops and the church to take sides in a situation of conflict in order to bring about peace:

> In this situation of conflict and antagonism, in which just a few persons control economic and political power, the church has placed itself at the side of the poor and has undertaken their defence. The church cannot do otherwise, for it remembers that Jesus had pity on the multitude.

Similarly, the Anglican Bishop Desmond Tutu has worked ceaselessly for justice as General Secretary of the South African Council of Churches, as parish priest to a church in the black township of Soweto and, since 1986, as Archbishop of Cape Town, metropolitan of the Anglican church in southern Africa.

Although Desmond Tutu and Oscar Romero came from very different backgrounds and their countries are a thousand miles apart, they preached the same message, that peace and reconciliation can only come with justice in a divided and unequal society. As Oscar Romero placed himself at the head of the voiceless majority, so has Desmond Tutu. As he said at Pretoria University in March 1981:

173

The church must be ever ready to wash the disciples' feet, a serving church, not a triumphalistic church, biased in favour of the powerless, to be their voices, to be in solidarity with the poor and oppressed, the marginalized ones – yes, preaching the gospel of reconciliation, but working for justice first since there can never be real reconciliation without justice. It will demonstrate in its very life that Jesus has broken down the wall of partition, and so in its common life there will be no artificial barriers to any Christian being able to participate fully.

*

These bishops share the agony and the hopes of their flock. And Archbishop Romero suffered for his people to the point of martyrdom. Such examples seem far removed from the life of a bishop in Brighton or Durham. On the other hand, we should not assume that it is 'easier' to be a bishop in comfortable surroundings. It may be *more* difficult to bring an affluent society to believe in spiritual values. We simply observe that if (as we believe) English bishops ought to become more obviously 'signs of contradiction', there are many examplars for them to follow on the inward journey that we now begin.

Part IV

Quo Vadis?

———

10

2001: An Episcopal Odyssey

So who should lead the English churches into the next millennium? What kind of bishops do we need? In what should they believe? Why should we believe in them? Anglican and Catholic bishops in the year 2001 will be leading, as shepherds, an ever increasing flock, but with fewer and fewer sheepdogs (priests). This will be a particular problem for the Catholic bishops. Indeed, it already is a problem in many parts of the world, most notably Africa and Latin America. There is not an unlimited supply of suitable candidates for the priesthood who are male and prepared to remain celibate. The Catholic church is having to acknowledge this, hence its recent return to the days of married deacons. It may be that the third millennium after Christ (well, perhaps the very end of that millennium: a thousand years is a short time in church politics) will see a return also to married priests and *bishops*, bringing the Catholic church into line with its Anglican brethren and into line with the origins of the episcopacy in the married fisherman Peter and his friends.

The problem of eligibility for Anglican bishops is a different one and, as we have seen, already upon us. There is no doubt that women bishops will become a significant feature of the Anglican church in the next decade, let alone the next millennium. That will take the Anglican church out of line with its Catholic brethren and with the male origins of the episcopacy. That in turn poses the question of whether the Anglican communion will fragment. That depends on the kind of leadership experienced by Anglicanism. We expect the next Archbishop of Canterbury to take a positive grip on such trends, if only by redefining 'communion' into a looser concept that allows diversity of practice to proliferate.

The present Pope constantly talks of the year 2000, as a significant event in the life of the church and the world. Younger, film-going generations will be preparing for odysseys in 2001. We believe that the turn of the century and the beginning of the new millennium will witness an explosion of nostalgia, but also of reassessment in all walks of life. We also believe that the Christian bishops will seize this opportunity to reconsider their faith and their role in their people's lives. The opportunity is heaven-sent to remind the world that Christ is so significant that we even date our years from the time of his birth (however inaccurate our counting).

We would welcome such a reconsideration of religion. We believe that it could be the occasion for challenging the myth that we are a secular society. The bishops have plenty of precedents for such a re-examination and they all point in the same direction, which we would describe as 'back to the future'.

If we take three giant figures from the early, middle and later life of the churches, for example, there is a unity in this aspect of their writings which transcends their disagreements. St Augustine, Martin Luther and Cardinal Newman could, we think, fairly be described as representative of their times and of distinctive approaches to Christianity. Suppose they could be brought back to give their opinions to a synod of bishops in the year 2000. What would their message be? Well, we know what their message was.

St Augustine of Hippo lived from AD 354 to 430. He was deeply influenced by the Bishop of Milan, St Ambrose, and himself became a bishop in Africa in the diocese of Hippo. He is often confused, by insular British Christians, with St Augustine of Canterbury, the first Archbishop of Canterbury in AD 597, sent by Pope Gregory the Great to refound the church in England.

St Augustine of Hippo found life as a bishop to involve confronting one heresy after another. For our purposes, perhaps the most relevant is the dispute with the Donatists. They were a schismatic group in the African church who refused to accept a bishop on the grounds that his consecrator had been a *traditor* (that is, someone who had surrendered his copy of the scriptures when Diocletian had forbidden their possession). St Augustine stressed that the unworthiness of a particular bishop did not affect the validity of the sacraments which he conferred, because their true minister was Christ.

He was himself a great bishop, on the model of the travelling road-show of today's papacy. He undertook about fifty journeys during his episcopacy, sometimes being away for months. It would have taken him nine days, for example, just to get to Carthage, which he visited some thirty times. But his people revered him as a pastor and he also found time to write an enormous number of works. In the words of the title of his most important book, he believed that the church constituted the 'City of God'.

His advice to today's bishops would be simple. You are not perfect, he would tell them (even though a later saint, Thomas Aquinas, considered bishops to be under a duty of perfection), but you are symbols of Christ, who is perfection. Keep true to the faith he entrusted to his apostles, your predecessors. Take his message, as he instructed, to his people. Immerse yourself in the scriptural accounts of the early church and build on that foundation to establish a modern City of God.

The bishops' repeated failure to do that and their obvious personal imperfections led to the Reformation. This is the term used to describe Christianity between the fourteenth and seventeenth centuries. Its leitmotif was the need for the church to return to its early excellence. If we focus on Martin Luther's central role at the beginning of the sixteenth century, this is clearly seen. For Luther liked to root his own work in that of St Augustine and St Paul. Luther was convinced that the church had departed from its apostolic and biblical foundations. Back to the future could have been his cry.

In particular, of course, Luther is significant for the topic of this book in so far as he castigated the excesses and abuses of the bishops of his day. Obedience to bishops is not necessary if they are disobedient to the Word of God in the Bible, he said.

His message to today's bishops would surely be the same. Do not be misled by intermediate mistakes, the accumulated failures of the church. Look instead to the examples of the very first apostles of Christ. If bishops are needed at all (which Luther, although not all Lutherans, disputed) they should help individual Christians come to terms with their faith and their God. Two thousand years on from Christ's birth, we must struggle to understand his significance in our lives.

John Henry Newman lived through the first nine decades of the nineteenth century, ultimately as a cardinal. His struggles to identify his own faith first as an Anglican then as a Roman Catholic and mostly in between as an Anglo-Catholic, encompass the story of the nineteenth-century bishops.

In particular, Newman lived through the time of the First Vatican Council's declaration of Papal infallibility and is famous for antici- pating its definition and yet not being in any hurry for its promulga- tion. Newman was happy to believe in Papal infallibility (at least in the second half of his life) *without* having it conclusively defined. This might bemuse non-believers who might well ask how one can believe in a doctrine which has not been defined. Newman spent much energy on explaining the nature of religious faith and belief, partly in answering that question.

Newman would be the last person to pretend that religious belief was easy to comprehend or to hold. His own doubts were evident. But he did not ignore the difficult questions. He confronted them. He also had the courage of his convictions. He would surely wel- come the Bishop of Durham's contemporary theological crusade. He would tell today's bishops that they are of no help to anyone or anything if they are not prepared to grapple with the deepest issues of religious belief. Other people can be social workers and poli- ticians. Only *holy* people should be bishops.

Suppose instead of assembling religious figures like Augustine, Luther and Newman we were able to witness a second 'Last' Supper between Christ and his apostles, but set in the year 2000. Christ would not be as worried by the media image of the next archbishops as many pundits are. But he would be concerned that his message should be taken to his people effectively. Christ believed that the humble people he chose would be transformed by that choice, by an outpouring of grace from the Holy Spirit.

But the Holy Spirit is certainly not spoilt for choice. He has his work cut out. Suppose you were choosing a new chief executive for the English operation of a multi-national company, or a new Prime Minister, or an ambassador or the executive director of an inter- national charity. Suppose also that your candidate was expected to have an extra dimension, the spirituality and humility of someone like Mother Teresa.

Then imagine that you disqualified all women, all married men, everyone under the age of fifty and over the age of sixty-five. If you further required that they must have spent their entire lives working on a variety of unrelated jobs, all unpaid (e.g. bishop's secretary, rector of a seminary, chaplain to the armed forces, possibly even a parish priest), then you would expect a small field of candidates.

That is the prospect facing the Catholic church in its search for a successor to Cardinal Hume. The head-hunting for the Anglican church's next leader is a little less demanding (non-celibates will be considered), but still difficult.

It is, we hope, obvious from this book that we believe that media speculation will be based on shifting sands (or stony ground) if it is merely a beauty parade or bookmaker's list of names. The way forward is, on the contrary, to identify what kind of leadership is needed. This requires an analysis of the role of bishops upon which we have embarked in this book, far more than an assessment of the merits of particular candidates.

Nobody stands out as the obvious successor to Basil Hume or to Robert Runcie. The options are, therefore, in each case to choose somebody who we hope will be transformed by the office or to transform the office so that it can be realistically undertaken.

As we have seen in an earlier chapter, the Pope has taken to appointing theologically conservative outsiders to important dioceses on the Continent. Some would say that he did that in England with the appointment of the Cambridge University Chaplain, Maurice Couve de Murville, to become Archbishop of Birmingham. A university chaplain at Sussex before Cambridge, with virtually no experience in normal parish life, he had the twin advantages of an establishment background and conservative theology. It would not be beyond the Pope's sense of doctrinal rigour to translate Couve de Murville to Westminster, although the appointment would be over the dead bodies of innumerable English clergy, bishops and laity. Of the other English archbishops, Worlock is too old and Michael Bowen of Southwark too reserved.

Moving down to the foot of the ecclesiastical ladder, two or three junior bishops are clearly being groomed for stardom, such as Bishop John Crowley, formerly secretary to Cardinal Hume and now one of his auxiliaries. A proto-bishop, Monsignor Vincent Nichols, is destined eventually to succeed Worlock as Archbishop of Liverpool (after all, he was Worlock's secretary, part of the pattern, and has for some time been the Secretary-General or Cabinet Secretary of the Bishops' Conference). David Konstant has already moved up a rung, from auxiliary bishop in Westminster to Bishop of Leeds (a see which may soon become an archdiocese). Chris Budd has been a popular pastor in his new diocese of

Plymouth and has the pedigree of an earlier job as rector of a seminary.

But the two front-runners are on the middle rungs. Cormac Murphy-O'Connor, formerly rector of a seminary (and in Rome, which scores extra points), has the attraction of combining attributes of both Cardinal Hume and his predecessor Cardinal Heenan. Like Hume he is from an establishment background. Like Heenan, and the majority of British Catholics, he is of Irish stock. He is the bookies' favourite.

Bishop Crispian Hollis is the likeliest alternative, worth at least an each-way bet. He is again an establishment figure (son of the MP, nephew of the spy accused in *Spycatcher* and elsewhere of being a double agent). He was Chaplain at Oxford University (the opposite number to the current Archbishop of Birmingham – the Oxbridge chaplaincies are worth the same as the rectorship of a seminary in scaling the ecclesiastical ladder). Above all, he is a great media man, formerly Assistant Head of Religious Affairs for the BBC; he looks good on screen and sounds good as the voice-over for religious events.

Of course, the next Archbishop of Westminster might be promoted straight from the ranks like Basil Hume (although the abbot of a Benedictine community has a quasi-episcopal status). A long-odds outsider would be Monsignor Jack Kennedy. Yes, of course, he is currently the rector of a seminary in Rome. Although he would be a better choice for the see of Liverpool, where he spent twenty-five years as a priest, Liverpool and London look pretty close when viewed from Rome. He would be a lively choice, combining a down-to-earth manner with a powerful intellect. Incidentally, he was ordained in Rome together with a life-long friend who would be leading the field had he stayed in the game: Anthony Kenny, who left the priesthood and became a distinguished Oxford scholar, Master of Balliol, Warden of Rhodes House and President of the British Academy. Those credentials would be perfect if only he were still a priest and/or could be certain that there is a God. Strictly speaking, of course, a cardinal does not have to have been a priest and, loosely speaking, many commentators seem unperturbed by agnosticism.

So Cormac Murphy-O'Connor, Crispian Hollis, John Crowley and Jack Kennedy will probably be the names referred for further sorting by the process we have outlined. Crispian Hollis and John Crowley would head a pastoral church, Cormac Murphy-O'Connor and Jack Kennedy a prophetic church. None could quite live up to Basil Hume's spirituality nor live down to his bureaucratic and organizational limitations. All have played a careful hand in political and social matters. All are ecumenically minded. All would be up to the job. On the most popular, cynical view of the Roman appointments system, then, the only problem is that the Pope might opt for someone else.

The obvious front-runner for the number-one job in the Church of England ought to be the number two, the Archbishop of York. Yet Dr Habgood has no prospect of moving to Canterbury. He is, by his own admission, a back-room boy. He is also too closely identified with Robert Runcie. It is time for a change. He is also too old, too strained in his relations with the Prime Minister, who has told friends she finds his sermons dull, and regarded as too distant by his laity and clergy.

What about the next rung of the ladder, the senior bishops? The Bishop of London received Mrs Thatcher's imprimatur first time round for his present diocese, but he has absolutely no chance of a second promotion. He is, as we have seen, too much of a right-wing prophet crying in the wilderness to be acceptable to the bulk of Anglicans. Equally, the other senior see, Durham, will not lose its bishop to Canterbury. David Jenkins is perceived to be far too much of a left-wing prophet and far too probing in his theology. Prophets are indeed without honour in their own country.

Talking of which, one attractive solution might be to choose a primate from a different part of the Anglican communion. After all, as we have seen, the Archbishop of Canterbury is an international leader. If so, the clear front-runners would be Desmond Tutu and Robert Eames. There would, however, seem to be no logic in removing Archbishop Tutu from Cape Town where he can do most good, even if his infectious enthusiasm could revitalize the Church in England. The rules would also have to be changed to deal with the problem of swearing an oath of allegiance to the Queen of England.

Archbishop Eames, on the other hand, is a fast-improving favourite to move to Canterbury. He already is, in word and deed, the effective head of international Anglicanism in the light of his report on women's ordination, which has calmed post-Lambeth nerves and pointed a way ahead on that most divisive of questions. Why not give this charming peacemaker the title to go with the function? Well, it may be easier for Eames to fulfil this important role *outside* the Church of England. Perhaps the functions of the Canterbury job need to split. Eames would make an ideal international Secretary-General of the Anglican communion of churches. But he would have his work cut out if he also had to give the Church of England spiritual leadership.

Does that leave David Sheppard as the prime contender? He could certainly expect to be offered York although he might prefer to stay in Liverpool. He would be a popular choice for Canterbury. Recent difficulties in English cricket prevent us from saying that if he was good enough to captain England at cricket, he should be able to captain the national religious team. But some critics feel he lacks the theological technique to open the batting for the Anglicans. Although we have discounted the direct influence of Prime Ministers, David Sheppard might appeal (if you will pardon the cricketing allusion) more to a Labour leader. With a change of government, Bishop Mark Santer of Birmingham could also come into the reckoning.

The man who has the fewest question-marks against him is probably Richard Harries, formerly Dean of King's College, London, a prolific writer and broadcaster and now the Bishop of Oxford. Like Eames, however, Harries has his critics who feel that he is too much the media man, although, as the late Gary Bennett pointed out in his notorious *Crockford*'s preface, a pleasing appearance on television can be a boost to chances of ecclesiastical preferment.

The favourite to succeed Robert Runcie as Archbishop of Canterbury, if the clergy or laity were allowed to vote, would be Bishop Carey of Bath and Wells. Why? Eighty per cent of the Church of England come from the low-church Protestant tradition, and Bishop Carey is one of the few of that ilk to have become a bishop in recent times. His theological credentials are impeccable as a former principal of Trinity Training College (back to the penchant for seminary rectors we noticed before).

As the election does not proceed in such a democratic way, however, the field is wide open. Our own impression is that Harries, Santer and Carey are the most talented English candidates, but the successor to Robert Runcie can only be determined when the question of the dual role of the Archbishop of Canterbury – the 'Eames factor' – has been decided.

And as we have stressed, it is that kind of question that needs to be resolved before a list of names has any real significance.

We all know that the Holy Spirit moves in mysterious ways his wonders to perform. Whatever the inspired choices as the next leaders of the British churches, we hope that a clear picture of the best kinds of bishop has emerged from this book. Bishops must, above all, be exemplars of Christianity in action and they must be prepared to ask the difficult questions of their own, and their followers', beliefs. A bishop with the prayerful spirituality of Cardinal Hume, the theological insight of the Bishop of Durham, and a combination of the Liverpool bishops' concerns for the voiceless and their ability to be effective voices, such a bishop would be our ideal model.

Index

Index

Index

Index

Index